"This book is an open, b
the life of a genuine per
her life. If you don't have a clue about your life, read this book. It
will help you realize that you are not alone in whatever obstacles
you incur, and you can also find your answer through faith."

Doris L. Graham
Entrepreneur

"My soul was enlightened and blessed all the while my heart wept
as I cheered. Bridget had no idea when she wrote this book that
she would inspire at least one person in her life, me. Imagine how
many others she will inspire. Those lost souls *Without a Clue* after
reading her story of faith, hope, prayer, determination, challenges
and love, will find the *Clue*."

Marilyn (Putt-Putt) Lawton-Jenkins
Philadelphia, PA

"Thank you, Lord! *Without a Clue* is your testimony of the love,
the mercy, the goodness and the grace that God is giving unto
you. *Without a Clue* clued in on the void that we experience in our
lives without Jesus Christ. Continue to give God all the honor,
praise and glory for all things. I love you and I Bless the name of
Jesus for you."

Mary I. Briggs
Philadelphia, PA

"The more I read, the more I was touched, and found myself saying, 'I was *Without a Clue*.' But, through Christ he gave Bridget
a chance to start over by mending her heart, healing her soul and
she broke through the afflictions by faith, which has inspired me
to trust in God who has a plan for all our lives. You have always
been my mentor, but now you're my inspiration."

Selma D. Cooper
Willingboro, New Jersey

WITHOUT A *Clue*

written by
Bridget Turner

WITHOUT A
Clue

*one woman's journey from
darkness into light*

TATE PUBLISHING & *Enterprises*

Without a Clue
Copyright © 2008 by Bridget Turner. All rights reserved.

This title is also available as a Tate Out Loud product. Visit www.tatepublishing.com for more information.

No part of this publication may be reproduced, stored in a retrieval system or transmitted in any way by any means, electronic, mechanical, photocopy, recording or otherwise without the prior permission of the author except as provided by USA copyright law.

Some names have been changed to respect peoples' privacy.

The opinions expressed by the author are not necessarily those of Tate Publishing, LLC.

Published by Tate Publishing & Enterprises, LLC
127 E. Trade Center Terrace | Mustang, Oklahoma 73064 USA
1.888.361.9473 | www.tatepublishing.com

Tate Publishing is committed to excellence in the publishing industry. The company reflects the philosophy established by the founders, based on Psalm 68:11,
"The Lord gave the word and great was the company of those who published it."

Book design copyright © 2008 by Tate Publishing, LLC. All rights reserved.
Cover design by Elizabeth A. Mason
Interior design by Steven Jeffrey

Published in the United States of America

ISBN: 978-1-60462-205-8
1. Inspirational: Motivational   2. Biography: Autobiography
07.11.06

dedication to my heavenly angels

I would like to dedicate my life story to my dearly missed effervescent oldest sister, Lisa Marie Jesse, who passed on February 10, 1998, on her son Terrance's sixteenth birthday, from cardiovascular disease and morbid obesity. Thank you for sharing my journey every day of my life, thirty-six years until your death. I didn't understand then why you had to go, but I am comforted knowing that you outwardly accepted Christ as your Lord and Savior and because I believe you made it to heaven, you're in a far better place, and hopefully, I will see you again!

To my daddy, William Edward Jesse, who passed on August 18, 2000, of lung cancer, for being a strong yet compassionate father, who did his best to instill the wisdom that I live with today, and who accepted Jesus Christ during his second marriage! My hope is that you understand, that as a Christian, I feel compelled to share our story to hopefully help someone else, and that my intention is not to embarrass myself or our family because as I shared my vision of *Without A Clue* during your lifetime, you still subscribed to the belief "what goes on in this family, stays in the family!" Unfortunately, if I keep silent about our story, my secrets/shame will be buried with me, and my hope is that others, and especially my children Mario and David III, will understand that the truth really does set us free!

To my former mother-in-law, Mary Elaine Bosman, who departed this life, but went on to heaven on April 20, 2005. My angel, Mrs. Bosman, was a private-duty nurse in the evenings, who would leave her over-night job and come straight to my hospital room to encourage me in my deep sorrow (depression), and I found comfort and strength in those daily visits because I had truly lost my way and felt so helpless and alone until you were there, and I know it was partially you who willed me to live again! Thank you for believing in me even before I believed in myself, and for always being there for innumerable heartfelt moments. You were the other mother I needed, and I'm proud to finally respond to your often asked question, "Are you on your computer yet?" "Yes, Mrs. Bosman, my memoir is finally complete!"

I never imagined that I would be living my life without you, Lisa, daddy, and Mrs. Bosman, physically beside me, so I carry each of you inside me every day to give me the strength, faith and hope that I will see you again.

acknowledgements

I would like to thank my husband, David Turner Jr., for supporting me through much adversity ("for better, for worse, in sickness and in health"), and who has demonstrated great strength and character and has risen to the occasion and stepped up when I needed him the most, during my illness! Anyone can make it through the wedding, but not everyone can survive a marriage! His endurance and strength have not only impacted me, but has captured my heart. Thank you, honey, I love you!

My eldest son Mario (my "Sweetie"), who at sixteen years of age became my life coach and comforter as we fought through huge crocodile tears together! He literally picked me up when I was down, encouraging me to fight through the pain and grief, reminding me that I was "his inspiration," willing me to want to live. He said, "Mommy, if you fail, I fail!"

And, also to my youngest son, David (my "Boob"), who

at three, opened my eyes and made me realize that he truly needed his mother, and I needed to hang in there for him as well. Unfortunately, he has already witnessed so much of my pain at such a tender age. My hope and prayer is that you have grown stronger because "the Lord puts no more on us than we can bear."

My mother, Geneva Jesse, for her constant loving care; stepmother; brother and sister, Geneis and Geneva; my cousin, Ernestine Stone, who is more like a sister to me; another cousin Lisa Brown (David III's Godmother); two very best friends in my world, Doris Graham and Marilyn (Putt-Putt) Jenkins (Mario's Godmother); Mary I. Briggs, my friend who became my dedicated caregiver introducing me to my church family, Enon Tabernacle Baptist Church in Philadelphia, Josephine Hayes, my friend who doesn't always tell me what I want to hear, but will always be treasured for the many acts of love and support, especially during my time of despair, Patricia Burt and Darcel Young, for their prayers, hospital and Rehab visits and for being there for me when times got really tough, Martha (Bea) Kilson for your matriarchal wisdom, care and encouragement. To Gwen Philips and Iris Roundtree, therapists, as well as your entire book club for the focus discussion held in my honor in 2005 in which you took time out of your schedules to offer invaluable feedback to an up and coming writer, helping me to arrive at the clue of "faith" I hadn't yet discovered. Remarkably, Gwen and I were both baptized on the same date, February 27, 2007, confirming my belief that God is supreme, and He should be my ultimate confidant, my Alpha and Omega! And, just so I don't miss anyone, thank all of you who prayed for me and are continuing to pray for me.

Table of Contents

13 . . . . Foreword by Deana E. Ferguson
23 . . . . Early Years — In My Sister's Shadow — Low Self Esteem (1972)
35 . . . . Geneva (Mommy) Has A Breakdown - Shame
39 . . . . William (Daddy) Has A Breakdown, Too! - Confusion
43 . . . . William And Geneva Jesse
55 . . . . Mario, The Good, The Bad, The Ugly (1973)
69 . . . . Marriage To Mario (1981)
81 . . . . How Do I Deal With A Spouse Addicted To Drugs? (1989)
87 . . . . Am I My Mother's Keeper?
91 . . . . "All The World's A Stage" Desire To Be A Corporate Star—
Reinvent Myself!
107 . . . . Financial Bondage: High End-Vehicles
111 . . . . Relationship With Suave Clark
115 . . . . Acceptance Of JesUs Christ As My Lord And Savior
117 . . . . Another Chance At Love —My Prince Charming (1997)
123 . . . . My Sister Lisa's Death (1998)
127 . . . . David Turner Iii's Birth (1998)
129 . . . . Yes, I Am My Mother's Keeper
133 . . . . Death Of My Daddy —William Jesse (2000)
137 . . . . When Are We Relocating?
141 . . . . Help, I Can't Walk! Loss Of Hope (2001)
185 . . . . Loss Of Three Fingertips — Repulsion And Shame (2003)
201 . . . . Mary Elaine Bosman (2005)
209 . . . . Finding The Clues
211 . . . . Spiritual Foundation—Leaving A Legacy
215 . . . . Confessing Lord As Savior - Baptism
219 . . . . Love God And Love Neighbor As Self—Most Important Pieces

223	Loving One Another-Family And Friends
229	Love Self - Developed Better Self Image
231	Hope And Faith — "As A Man Thinketh" Crippled Physically (Faith In Jesus)
233	Truth-Sharing My Testimony - Increasing My Territory
237	Better Steward Of What God Has Given
241	God Has A Plan, "Ordered My Steps"
243	My Heart's Desire
247	Epilogue

foreword

I have always considered myself a well read person. Reading for me is therapeutic. It helps me to relax, and often times, imagine myself half way around the world. I have learned so much from books. However, I must admit that I have never experienced a book as personally as this one.

I have been acquainted with Bridget Turner for most of my life. I can remember when I was about sixteen; Bridget bought a brand new camaro with a T-top. She came to my house to take me for a ride in it. It was a warm day. She had the top off, and we were cruising around town. I remember thinking that Bridget had a great life. She had a good job, and a hot car. I was completely unaware of what her life was really like.

Bridget worked with my mom at a local utility company. Over the years, they had become very close. I sometimes wondered why Bridget was drawn to my mother who is much older than she. I now believe that it was because she saw my mom as a wise, mature woman.

When Bridget was first hospitalized, my mom told me that she couldn't walk. I was shocked at this news. Unfortunately, that was only the beginning for her. Over the next couple of years, my mother would update me on Bridget's condition. She spent a great deal of time at the hospital with Bridget, praying for her, and encouraging her to be strong and trust God. I was blown away by all that she was going through. The first time I saw Bridget after her diagnosis, she came to my home for a barbeque. I hardly recognized her. She didn't look like the Brdiget I knew. She was walking ever so slowly with leg braces on, and she was half the size that she used to be; but she had this aura of strength and determination about her. I think it was at that momtn that I realized that this woman had claimed victory in Jesus, and over the disease that sought to destroy her, even though her journey to a "healthy" life was far from over.

Without a Clue is the journey of a most courageous spirit. A spirit that ultimately never gave up, even though at times it seemed the easiest thing to do. This is a story that I know was a painful one to share with the world. I also know that it is a story that had to be told. As I turned the pages, I found myself crying for the child who had to deal with two mentally ill parents. I cried for the youn woman who tried so hard to keep her marriage and family together. I got angry at the drugs that ruled her first husband's life. I rejoiced in her finding her second husband and soulmate, David Turner, Jr.; man that would have his matrimonial bond tested within the first three years of marriage.

Without a Clue is a renewal of hope, faith and love. It is a testament to the healing power of forgiveness and the abundance of compassion. After taking this literary journey, you will be touched by its raw truthfulness, and changed by its constant reminder that things are not always what they seem.

Bridget, I honor your heroism and strength. You are truly a gifted writer. Thank you for having the courage to tell your story.

— Deana E. Ferguson

"WEEPING MAY GO ON ALL NIGHT, BUT JOY COMES WITH THE MORNING!" (PSALMS 30:5 NLT)

preface

Without a Clue was originally conceptualized three decades ago in a freshman English class at my alma mater, Martin Luther King High School (MLK), Philadelphia, Pennsylvania, in 1975 when I was just fourteen years old. Our assignment was to read autobiographies of famous African-Americans, Booker T. Washington, Sojourner Truth, Harriet Tubman, etc., and then write our very own autobiographies. This was a particularly daunting challenge for me, but truly cathartic, because at the time I felt like a "nobody," however, it forced me to think about "Bridget" for once in my lifetime and not my sister, Lisa, whose shadow I lived under, but who I was as an individual.

Unfortunately, I hit a major stumbling block because of my shame and fear of disclosing too much of myself. I was a fourteen-year-old adolescent, extremely shy, suffering from low self-esteem, and frankly cared about the opinions of my peers. I was ashamed because both of my parents were committed involuntarily to mental institutions, and afraid that I would be unjustly labeled "crazy" by my teacher and/or classmates if I were to provide truthful information pertaining to them. I felt very alone with my dilemma, thinking that I was the only teenager in the world living in crisis with major family difficulties.

At that time, I imagined my classmates' home lives were far better than mine, and oh, how I wished I could trade places with them! Inwardly I felt depressed and frequently had bouts where I wished I were dead! I thought about ending my life by taking pills and quietly sleeping forever, but I couldn't do it because my spirit wouldn't allow me! I spent countless hours worrying that my family's secret would be discovered and I would be ridiculed because some of my peers could be so insensitive and downright cruel. There was always a group of kids "bussing" (saying mean things) about someone's momma!

I anguished long and hard about what I would disclose and managed to write my autobiography omitting "the mental challenges of my parents" and to my delight I received an excellent grade, an "A". My teacher and classmates were never the wiser, and never did learn my truth or shame! While I kept my painful secrets to myself, I discovered I truly enjoyed writing because it gave me a voice and a chance to express myself, especially because I was so withdrawn. I found writing to be such a powerful way to express myself and a calming release for my emotions, truly therapeutic.

My passion for writing continued in college, and by far English became my favorite subject! I excelled when we were required to write essays because I discovered the secret ingredient to win over most any professor's heart—I always shared personal stories that I felt comfortable disclosing, but still I couldn't bring myself to share the painful fact that my parents literally went "crazy"! I was astutely aware that some subjects were simply taboo, and mental illness was one of them! As we read each other's writings, I noticed that my classmates never really shared topics of much value to me nor disclosed anything which could have seemed derogatory in any way. Everyone pretended like their home lives were picturesque.

However, I felt like a prisoner to my shame, hiding in the dark behind my family's secrets. We moved from the "projects," lost our home in a sheriff's sale, both my parents went "crazy!" Why my family? I would ask myself, "Why am I feeling ashamed?" I did nothing to cause this humiliation! After all I was just a minor, yet I was feeling so disconnected and estranged from my peers because they couldn't feel my pain nor relate to what I was feeling emotionally.

Fortunately, I am older and have acquired a bit more knowledge about life and people, and have discovered we're all in the same boat, but everyone is fighting his own battle. What I have learned about living is that trouble comes to us all at various intervals in our lives and is often our best teacher.

Mental illness and the secrecy that surrounds it happens in many families, including some of those very peers, but remaining silent about it, or any troubling scenario, for that matter, kept me in bondage! As the saying goes, "We are as sick as our secrets." In addition I have discovered that the more I conceal, the worse I feel...

In a sense, I am rewriting my high school autobiography from a more enlightened and mature perspective, if you will. Intrinsically I feel a correlation between living with my secrets, fears, and pretensions as unnecessarily shameful, kept me emotionally in bondage, isolated from others, and prevented me from sincerely connecting with those who may be in or have been in similar type situations.

As opposed to sharing the truth regarding my experiences to intentionally help myself as I help others live more meaningful and purpose filled lives, I believe disclosing the truth is therapeutic and healing, and hopefully help others overcome their own challenges! A wonderful illustration of this concept is the portrait of a strong arm reaching down to pull a less fortunate hand up. It is an inspiring image that has left an indelible impression in my mind's eye.

We each have stories of triumphing in this world we live in, and as a way to share our wisdom and insight, I truly believe in the idea of mentoring, which can be defined as "teaching or coaching." I have enjoyed mentoring several inner-city at risk students to expose them to the working world, and I have myself been mentored.

I feel compelled to share my secrets with others because I believe that revealing my secrets will free my soul. Today I have chosen to release all shame and live my life out loud and with intention and show up as my authentic self. As writer IyanlaVanzant writes in *Until Today*, "You cannot live out loud if you are hiding behind what was. Living out loud means acknowledging my shortcomings and celebrating my strengths. It means that you let people know exactly who you are and expect them to be as thrilled as you are about who you are." After all, In order to grow, flowers require both sunshine and rain.

"One evening an old Cherokee told his grandson about a battle that goes on inside people. He said, 'My son, the battle is between two wolves inside us all. One is Evil. It is anger, envy, jealousy, sorrow, regret, greed, arrogance, self-pity, guilt, resentment, inferiority, lies, false pride, superiority, and ego. The other is good. It is joy, peace, love, hope, serenity, humility, kindness, benevolence, empathy, generosity, truth, compassion and faith.'

The grandson thought about it for a minute and then asked his grandfather, 'Which wolf wins?'

The old Cherokee simply replied, 'The one you feed.'"

- Author Unknown

SSH MENTAL ILLNESS IN FAMILY

CHAPTER I

EARLY YEARS — IN MY SISTER'S SHADOW — LOW SELF ESTEEM (1972)

As I reminisce about my childhood, the year was 1972, and my older sister, Lisa, and I were happy adolescents passionate and excited about life! We grew up in North Hills, Pennsylvania, a black suburban community, located just outside of Philadelphia. Although we lived in the projects, we were bussed to Sandy Run Elementary School, a predominately white school in Dresher, Pennsylvania, where a large portion of the population was Jewish, and where we were exposed to a better life. The school we attended was beautiful, clean and extremely well-funded—a far cry from the poor neighborhood schools we later attended in Philadelphia. Because of the large Jewish enrollment, we celebrated all the Jewish holidays, including Hanukah where we lighted the menorah and ate matzo balls. Our school had its very own planetarium, unlike any city school I know of. I remember we sometimes took class trips to our classmate's homes where many of them still had black maids and nannies, and big gorgeous swimming pools, a far cry from the North Hills projects where we returned to on the bus at the end of the day.

But, nevertheless, we were both really bright girls. At age eleven I was an introverted tomboy, and the complete opposite of my sister Lisa. Lisa was a year older brown-skinned, extroverted and already developing into a beauty. She was articulate and could do most anything she set her mind to! Boy, she could draw beautifully, sing and dance. She danced so well she and one of our friends, Debbie Russell, danced together on the now defunct Georgie Woods Show. She was also the apple of our dad's eye, and he classified Lisa as his pet, while I was just the baby, and I wasn't at all too happy with daddy's distinction between us. The statement made me feel envious, and caused division because I came to think he cared more for Lisa than me, and boy did I try to rub my dad's nose in his statement every chance I got! Nevertheless, I was my sister's shadow, and you never saw me without Lisa.

Growing up in North Hills was wonderful! Lisa and I thought we were wealthy because we never wished for anything we didn't get. Daddy, William Jesse, was a maintenance man—in other words someone who cleaned buildings, aspiring to do more with his life, and any time you'd ask him what he did he disguised his job title to portray something more, that he was proud of (maintenance engineer, environmental services, etc.). At that time the job he did was a bit of an embarrassment to Lisa and me. However, there was no greater dad as far as we were concerned! He was an excellent provider and there was absolutely nothing else we desired—nothing! However, he pampered Lisa with more expensive gifts and clothing than me and our mother, and I always thought it was because she resembled him so much. The two of them could have been twins, and it appeared that he just spit her out! They had the same skin tone, as well as, beautiful brown colored cat-eyes. Lisa had a thick, healthy head of hair which she styled just perfectly, while my hair was thin and resembled cotton, she often teased! To say I wasn't jealous would be an understatement! I was envious of all the attention she got from my dad, but like most big sisters, she was my hero.

From as long as I can remember, Lisa became my super hero! I remember one day when Lisa and I were four and three respectively. We were jumping on our beds playing, but Lisa was nearest to the window of our tiny home. She plummeted out the open window and fortunately landed on our clothesline where mommy had been hanging our clothing out to dry. Thank God for that clothesline because that's what saved her life! Her right arm caught hold of the clothesline, breaking it in a few places. She was rushed to Abington Memorial Hospital where a cast was set on her arm. News spread rapidly about Lisa's fall, especially because it had been a nice summer day and many of our neighbors in our tight knit community were outside and witnessed Lisa "flying out the window." Thus, she was dubbed a superhero, "Superman" at four years old. Everyone put their signatures on Lisa's cast!

I adored my big sister and she loved and protected me! However, from before I could remember I felt like the black sheep of our family, like perhaps I had been adopted. I had a light-complexion, unlike my sister or parents, with short kinky hair, and was called "bald-head" by Lisa on more times than I choose to remember, but mostly we argued about stupid, sister things! My feelings were always crushed, but I would get my little licks in by retaliating and calling her "crooked teeth" because although she was beautiful, her bottom teeth went in and out, and she could have benefited from a pair of braces, instead of the lavish clothing our dad chose to purchase for her! I was a tomboy with short-hair, and that distinction was sufficient for me, until I hit puberty and boys were a bit cruel and seemed to take notice of us girls, and sometimes mistook me for a boy, and of course Lisa was the person who reported what these boys said.

Because Lisa was the favorite daughter to my dad, our mother, Geneva, attempted to compensate and help me feel better, but mommy was definitely lacking mothering sensitivity, and would often say something negative and hurtful like, "Girl, pinch your nose," and I believed because I had a thick nose, unlike white girls, my nose was too large, and I'd immediately sink inside. She made the comment enough times for me to question her motive. Why would she say such a hurtful thing, and she replied, "Your nose is too wide!" Wow, what a blow to my esteem. She attempted to undo what she said, but once someone makes a statement to a child, it's difficult to change the interpretation.

My self esteem suffered because quite frankly "I wasn't pretty enough" in the eyes of my family. I used to ask my parents whether I had been adopted or whether my dad was actually my father, but they always replied, "Yes." Fortunately, God gave me a few curves (hips) and my turning point came when boys started noticing me, and my first love (boyfriend) seemed to absorb everything I despised about my appearance.

Another reason for my low self-esteem was being raised in the projects, and attending a predominantly white, wealthy school district for my primary education, and being exposed to our parents' faulty opinion, that somehow "white people were somehow better than blacks" helped me develop an inferiority complex. I developed the belief that white people were intellectually better than I was because daddy often bragged about the ability of various white friends he knew, but I had to overcome this stereotype because it didn't serve me well.

My parents were really good-hearted parents. Daddy was an excellent provider and mom was really good at nurturing us, however, they didn't go to church, and they didn't know God, but they did send us to church with our maternal grandmother, who insisted on our attending most every Sunday. Grand mom Morn, Lucille Fitzgerald, Stone, Pace (10/6/16–1/12/89) was born in Danville, Virginia and relocated to Willow Grove (Crestmont), Pennsylvania, the area where most of my relatives and I call home. She was born to Georgina Boxdale Fitzgerald and Monroe Fitzgerald and was one of thirteen siblings, eight girls and five boys, all deceased except one girl, Lena (Lonnie) Grasty, who resides in a nursing facility. Following is a list of all siblings from eldest to youngest along with their offspring, as told to me by my uncle Lewis Stone, my mom's eldest brother:

Eight Girls:

Summer Fitzgerald Grasty with a whopping seventeen children: Alice, Rubin (Ribbon), Hilda Sue (deceased); Earlie (deceased), Beatrice, Bob, Wayne; Main (deceased), Buck (deceased) Thomas (Blue) was a twin, that died at birth, Mildred (deceased)

Hopper, Luther (deceased), Dorothy (Dot), resides in Virginia, Delores, J.C. (deceased) Matilda (Tilly)– died in New York and buried their mom, C. C. Jean (deceased) and Carol,

Frances Fitzgerald Kent had five children: Sally, Willie, Charles, Elizabeth (Lizzy) and Shirley,

Sis Fitzgerald Jones of Chester, Pennsylvania, four children: Elsie, Johnny, Snooky and Sonny all deceased

Leticia (Pig) Fitzgerald Womack and had two daughters: Helen Lewis and Dolly Mae Womack Taylor (deceased)

Eva Fitzgerald Saunders, six children: James, Clarence (Nutty) Jr. (deceased), Richard (deceased), Doris Jean, Charles (Leftie)–(deceased). Stanley (Bike)

Lucille Fitzgerald Stone Pace, eight children: Dolly, Barbara (deceased), Lewis, Albert (Burton)–(deceased), Geneva, Leonard Ray, Glenn and Larry;

Lena (Lonnie) Fitzgerald Grasty, only living sibling with nine children: Shirley (deceased), Mable, John, Thomas (deceased), Frances, Margaret, Ann (deceased), Terrie Lee (passed in a truck accident), and Sandy;

Gladys (Lee) Fitzgerald Grasty, Betty, handicapped son (passed young), Charles (Shotgun) Grasty (deceased), James (Dick)-(deceased), Carter (deceased) and Gladys (Tata)

Five Boys

Alphonso (Jill) Fitzgerald of Danville, Virginia and

had three children, Alphonso (Scrap) Fitzgerald, Jr. (deceased), Patricia (Pat) Mayo (deceased), Dave (King) Fitzgerald;

Penn Fitzgerald of Chester, PA, no children;

Dave Fitzgerald and had five daughters, Ellen Ann, Louise, Janice, Ruby Mae and Linda;

James (Dock) Fitzgerald, no children;

Jeff Fitzgerald, no children

Morn had a passion for Christ, and established her very own storefront church, the United Church of the First Born located on Bringhurst Street in the Germantown section of Philadelphia, Pennsylvania, which she purchased from the city of Philadelphia for $1. It was a small church which contained lots of love. At church Morn was known as Mother Pace.

On Sundays she would gather all of us grandchildren together, and load us up in her brand new blue station wagon, even though she couldn't drive. She would have either our step grandfather, Bishop Leroy Pace, or one of her older grandsons; usually cousin Tony Stone would transport us, along with some neighbors and friends to church. We would have church all day long on Sunday beginning with Sunday school and continue for the duration of the day. Sunday school was normally taught by Ernestine (Tine) Stone, one of our favorite cousin's or Cynthia Robinson (Tine's best friend). We would have the most delightful Christmas and Easter programs, where we would have to sing and recite Bible verses. My favorite, "For God so loved the world that he gave his only Son, so that everyone who believes in him will not perish but have eternal life. God did not send his

Son into the world to condemn it, but to save it" (John 3:16–17 NLT).

Morn's weekly ritual was to begin preparing her yummy Sunday dinners beginning on Saturday evening, which I highly anticipated! I would sit there hoping to sample a taste of the cake batter and trying to absorb as much as possible, and sometimes she'd allow me to help her bake. On Sunday, she'd leave a portion of the meal home, and a few of her sons would complain, "You always take the good food to church." My grandmother sponsored the most memorable bus trips to Coney Island and Ocean City, New Jersey, packing some of her delectable fried chicken, cakes, peaches and plums.

MOM'S (GENEVA) BEGINNING

Geneva, our mother, was born on 7/16/43 at home in Danville, Virginia, Pittsylvania County and delivered by a midwife named Fannie Logan. Her given name is Mary Anna Stone, a name selected for her by a Caucasian woman, who was a friend of her mothers', in exchange for simply a baby outfit. A small price to pay for a name! However, she chose to be called Geneva, named after one of her mother's favorite sisters, Eva. Her parents were Lucille (Morn) Fitzgerald and Eziel (Witt) Stone. She had seven siblings: Dorothy Huff, Barbara Stone (deceased), Lewis Stone, Albert Stone (deceased), Geneva Jesse, Leonard Raymond Stone, Glenn Stone and Larry Stone. Mom was a homemaker and boy was she beautiful! She was brown-skinned and wore a long fall wig which seemed so natural that everyone mistook it for her very own hair. She wore makeup and manicured long nails she kept painted a vibrant red. Geneva took great care of her home and her children. We were a beautiful family, and if you were to have taken a poll at that time, I believe many thought we would succeed as a family.

Lisa and I participated at the local recreation center in the dance and singing contests. However, Lisa was the true performer, while I usually pretended to sing. We often sang Peaches and Herb's song, "Two Little Kids," and received standing ovations. We participated in many of the challenging spelling bee contests as well, where I normally excelled.

Our relatives in Philadelphia had nicknames for us because we remembered everything, they would sometimes jokingly say, "If you don't want something repeated, you should not say anything around those two "walking encyclopedias!"

Yes, life was good at the Jesse residence. Meals were provided three times per day, and our clothing was always up-to-date and stylish because Wm. Jesse took great pride in the appearance of his family! He took us shopping during every holiday and during winter and spring breaks. For Christmas we made lists of what we wanted, and our Santa (Wm. Jesse) always delivered, even if he had to max out his credit cards in the process! Up until this point life seems to be a fairytale!

Daddy, being the consummate dreamer, decided to move us out of the comfort of the North Hills Projects to expose us to a better life, similar to the Jefferson's theme song "moving on up to the big times." We moved into our very first home at 7963 Temple Road in Mount Airy, Philadelphia, Pennsylvania. It was a beautiful modern row home with central air conditioning, garbage disposal, washer and dryer, and to top it off we each had our very own bedrooms! Lisa's room had purple carpeting and a sewing machine, while my room was somewhat smaller with royal blue carpeting, a typewriter and fancy white shutters. We thought life couldn't get any better!

Unfortunately, our lives were about to change and the bliss and security we felt as children was about to be shaken and changed forever, gone was our childhood.

I think daddy bit off a little more than he could chew! Living in the projects was a breeze financially, but down on Temple Road the mortgage was steeper than he was used to paying, and to top it off he was the only person in the household working, and those Christmas spending sprees caught up to him and the creditors wanted their money ASAP!

Our mom, Geneva, had never really worked anywhere for long. She had sporadic part-time jobs working at Trestle's Cookie Factory, a small local dry cleaners doing piece work occasionally with our dad, a job cleaning hotel rooms at Lucky Well Motel, and English Village. She enjoyed the work, but they didn't pay much, and they hardly ever called her in, and definitely didn't include any benefits. Unfortunately, she didn't take the initiative, like daddy did, and expected to be cared for, and to her detriment. She was the proverbial homemaker, and unfortunately content in that roll!

Well, in 1973 daddy lost his job and sought other employment to try to meet his financial obligations, but the job he took only paid half of what he was used to earning. His behavior changed dramatically! He became short-tempered and withdrawn, and focused on all the problems in his life. Before we knew it, Christmas arrived and he had nothing to put under the tree as he had in previous years. But, instead of sitting us down and discussing the situation, he promised us the world and everything in it. He began fabricating and telling me and Lisa that "This is going to be the best Christmas yet," and is convinced that he can do and buy anything!

At this point, he has begun professing to be the Savior of the world (Christ Jesus). But, then Christmas arrives and there are no presents, and need I say, we are terrified! We have no idea what this could possibly mean for us so we cling to hope for the future and each other because we haven't a clue as to what's next.

Up until this point we, along with out mommy, Geneva, had been spoiled rotten and sheltered from the realities of a sometimes harsh, cruel world. We depended on our daddy to make everything wonderful and that he did! All of a sudden we're confused and uncertain as to what to expect next. We question our father, crying and nagging and asking for explanations. He can't explain he can only spurt out imagined information about the end of the world and promises for the future! This is the beginning of the nightmare for us.

Meanwhile, mommy becomes withdrawn, afraid, and very fragile because she can't help out financially because she has no saleable skills because she didn't complete high school because she dropped out of school when she became pregnant with Lisa. Consequently, she feels she can't find employment and decides to keep her troubled situation to herself, deciding to ride the waves of life alone. She had family, but she didn't turn to them because of her foolish pride.

Our parents began having more frequent arguments. The bills were not getting paid, creditors started calling, months go by and they fight constantly! During one of their frequent fights, Geneva threw hair remover (lye) on William's head which instantly gave him a gigantic bald patch causing him to shriek with pain and called him all types of expletives, and that was the last time we saw our dad for months. We were, however, hearing horrid tales of our father wandering in the streets and loitering in the bowling alley of Willow Grove, or directing traffic and appearing to think his name was Jesus.

Meanwhile, mom was trying to hold our family together, but then she couldn't handle the pressure of life. I remember going away for a weekend back to North Hills to visit our old friends, and boy are we unprepared for our lives when we returned.

It was scary, like a segment straight out of *the Twilight Zone*! When we arrived, our mom was somehow changed, yet we couldn't immediately put our fingers on what it was that changed in her because we were excited to be home. Until I entered the bathroom and noticed our clothing had been hand-washed and eerily hung all over the bathroom, as if we didn't own a washer and dryer.

CHAPTER II

GENEVA (MOMMY) HAS A BREAKDOWN - SHAME

Mom was disillusioned and screaming something about "the former Mayor Green being an evil man," and our family doctor whom we adored being a bad man as well! She's stating the newscasters (especially Walter Conkrite) is talking to her through the television set, and spurting out that she is white, "and Lisa and Bridget you are as well," and to top it off, she is forbidding us from hanging out with any of those black people, "because they're not your kind."

And, fortunately, one of my best friends, Marilyn (Putt), was dark-skinned, and seemed so mature for her age, and seemed to ignore my mom's insults, thank God. Marilyn later shared that she and her family knew another woman who had been mentally ill when she lived in North Philadelphia, and that's why she knew to ignore her, and I'm sure her mother coached her on this.

We wondered whether we would go to sleep, and awaken

safe in our beds away from this nightmare that was demolishing our lives! Everything seemed so bizarre, like something straight out of Alfred Hitchcock.

Fortunately, Lisa and I had each other, and Grandma Morn lived only a few miles from us in West Oak Lane and we decided to break our immediate family's secret by running, not walking to Grandma Morn hysterically, asking for guidance. Of course, Morn came to assist us on many occasions and was rejected by her very own daughter, which we couldn't understand.

For some unknown reason, our mom denied that Morn was her mother, opting to call her Lucille disrespectfully. We felt so ashamed and bewildered by our mom's outbursts and refusal of help that we so obviously needed we were left dumbfounded. While Geneva refused the assistance and threw the canned good items and cash in the waste paper basket, we secretly accepted all the food and money we could get from Morn. We ignored our mom's apparent mental condition, and tried to continue to go on with our lives in spite of mom, acting as if life were normal, when it was anything but!

I can recall vividly a few times our electricity was shut off for non-payment of service because we could not afford to pay the supplier. During those times, we lit candles just to see in the dark. Or like the time when the gas was shut off, we used our stove to heat our house.

Our maternal grandmother was quite a strong woman! She was the matriarch of our family, and assisted all of her children/grandchildren as much as she could. She was a domestic worker and continued cleaning white folks' homes until she died in 1989 to provide a living and put food on the table.

We attended school with the lunch money provided by Grandma Morn, and walked to school with our friends/classmates, Marilyn (Putt) Jenkins, Thomasina Martina, and Debbie Russell, just to name a few. Mommy would follow us to school, and because Marilyn's skin tone is dark, Mommy would attempt to shoo her away from us. So blatantly mistaken, all of a sudden she turned "white" and we did as well.

Life was becoming more and more nightmarish! We would sometimes return home and our green living room furniture would be covered with white unbleached flour. The color green, like the former Mayor Bill Green, was apparently evil, according to mom in her obviously disillusioned state, and the color brown was to be avoided at all costs because the color, like our family doctor, Dr. Brown, was taboo, and was not to be trusted. Lord, what were we to do? We were so embarrassed and didn't know which way to turn, except to pretend our lives were normal!

It got to the point where we weren't allowed to watch television because Geneva thought the newscasters (John Facenda, etc.) were talking to her and could make things happen, like casting spells on us right through the television set. There were times when she would be so enraged that she would literally be cursing the television set out. She would be cussing and waving her fingers, and saying, "Get your eyes out of here, we don't want any of your kind in here, I'm going to take something and bash your head in, if you keep on with that talk, something's going to happen," as she lashed out in a fit of frenzy.

Although I was forever the shy one, together with Lisa, we were very outgoing and sociable kids, and our friends often stopped by just to pay us a visit or picked us up to hang-out. However, our behavior changed abruptly once our mom began acting like an imposter, talking incessantly regarding topics that weren't even true and scaring us silly! We were terrified that everyone would find out about her, and bewildered as to how something like this could happen.

She started throwing our clothing out, anything that had a hint of green or brown in it! What would we wear to school? Temporarily during that summer our dad was unable to provide, Lisa and I began a little stint of shoplifting at the now defunct clothing store Corvette's and we attempted to bring our stolen summer shirts into the house, but they were unfortunately thrown away by our mom, not because they were stolen merchandise, but simply because many of the items had either green or brown in them.

Life was becoming unbearable and with the assistance of our maternal grandmother, we concocted a story to have her involuntarily committed to a psychiatric hospital because she was definitely not acting like herself. Unfortunately, she had to be endangering herself or someone else, and not just acting bizarrely. Our grandmother called the police and had her daughter/our mother committed because we felt that she was endangering a neighbor because we said, "She was throwing stones at her" Fortunately our plan worked and she was committed to Northwestern Mental Hospital for evaluation and help (treatment). It wasn't until years later that we thought we knew why she had the breakdown in the first place.

CHAPTER III
───────────────

WILLIAM (DADDY) HAS A BREAK-
DOWN, TOO! - CONFUSION

While Geneva was hospitalized, we stayed with Grandma Morn until William (daddy) returns to take us back home to Temple Road. We don't know where our dad has been all these months while we've been living through this nightmare, but he's daddy, and daddy will make everything all better, right?

Life takes on a weird sort of feeling, and we are becoming somewhat uncomfortable with our daddy's behavior. He would oftentimes walk around with his private areas exposed, or stare at us as if we were women and not "his little girls." It was a little awkward because we were just kids, and mommy was far away getting help for her condition!

One day daddy decided that he wanted a fat, juicy steak, and asked Lisa to prepare it for him. She acquiesced, but then suddenly, out of no where, William reaches for and grabs my breasts, but then I screamed, "What are you doing?" He quickly dismisses me and sends me outside! Fortunately, he wasn't really after me anyhow, he wanted Lisa...I objected, but he was dad, and respecting dad's demand, I reluctantly went and waited on the pavement, nervously awaiting my older sister's presence! After some time, seconds, minutes, perhaps a half hour later, Lisa bolts out the front door saying that he put his hands up her leg and fondled her. We anxiously discussed our dad's disgusting behavior and were afraid to return home, so instead we called our beloved Grandma Morn and she along with our Aunt Dolly Huff of Willow Grove escorted us to the police station to file charges against our dad for sexual molestation .That was the very first time I heard that expression, "sexual molestation." Our daddy was only locked up temporarily, because we decided not to formally press charges against him—after all he was our dad and had to be mentally disturbed! He was released on his own recognizance.

Several months later, daddy was arrested for loitering, directing traffic, and pretending to be God. Apparently, when he didn't take his prescription medication for his condition, he would hallucinate and become someone he wasn't. At these times he would tell us about all the toys and clothing he would buy us, and have elaborate, detailed ideas about how he was going to "make changes in the world!" We began noticing that at these times he just wouldn't sleep, but would instead pace the floors. During these occasions, it was extremely difficult to sleep peacefully because my imagination was in overdrive, and we were already living a surreal existence with him playing "God." A few times he was caught standing butt naked, hovering over Tine as she slept.

Grandma Morn became legal guardian of us while her

daughter Geneva and son-in-law William were hospitalized for their mental conditions. She received (DPA) public assistance from the state of Pennsylvania to care for us, of which she allotted us $15.00 every two weeks as an allowance. Lisa and I really looked forward to receiving our own money (1) because this was the first time we had our own money to spend the way we wanted, and (2) because we were able to purchase all the junk food and penny candy we desired from the corner store. Through all the sadness and uncertainty, Lisa and I had each other!

Several months passed and our family home at 7963 Temple Road was boarded up and padlocked, as if our family had been criminals, and the sign read "Sheriff's Sale." For sometime after, Lisa and I were embarrassed by this, but hey, it wasn't our fault if our parents couldn't continue to pay our mortgage. Our first home was sold for non-payment of the mortgage and back taxes. We were devastated, but fortunately our grandmother made a place for us in her already overcrowded home

Wow! What was happening? Was it true? Were we living a nightmare or were both our parents berserk? Why us? Will our lives ever be the same? And is this our inheritance?

DARKNESS

FEAR PAIN

CONFUSION

SADNESS

LOST

SECRETS

QUIET

ANGER

HIDING

CHAPTER IV

WILLIAM AND GENEVA JESSE

My dad, William Wilford (Edward) Jesse, born 4/17/36, was the third of eleven children (John, Jimmy, William, Jake, Henry, Morris, Leroy, Richard, Amanda (Doll), Evelyn (Daisy) and Pumkin) born to the late Amanda Jesse in Culpepper, Virginia, (Madison County) but grew up on Davisville Road in Willow Grove, Pennsylvania. He was educated in the Upper Moreland School District, and suffered from epilepsy (a neurological condition that can produce brief disturbances in the brain's electrical functions) which manifested itself through grand-mal seizures (generalized convulsions), which he never openly discussed even inside our family. However, we (mom, Lisa and I) whispered about dad's medical condition to one another in hushed tones because of our shame.

Apparently, daddy's seizures (as told to me by my dad) began as an infant when he developed a brain infection as a result of medicine administered by his mother, Amanda

Jesse. He was treated with anticonvulsant drugs, and spent some time residing at the Elwyn Institute, formerly Elwyn School, in Delaware County, a human services organization for people with special challenges, including developmental, physical and emotional disabilities, as well as those with disadvantages, but all that didn't matter because Lisa and I adored our dad beyond belief!

He was also hospitalized numerous times in his lifetime for mental illness (manic depression) at Duffers, Norristown State and Friend's Hospitals, after having bouts where he would stay up for days at a time, pacing the floors, ranting and raving professing to be God. During his first marriage, he wandered off, and told his physician, Dr. Charles Brown, "that he couldn't remember where he had been for an entire weekend." Dr. Brown admitted him to Duffers Hospital in Montgomery County.

Once he was arrested, it was usually determined that he wasn't in his "right mind" and he was transferred to the nearest mental hospital, wherever his records were, or wherever there was a bed. He normally was arrested and ended up being transferred to a mental hospital/institution.

We kept our dad's mental condition a secret from our friends because we were ashamed of his bizarre behavior and didn't know how they would respond. We had just recently relocated to Philadelphia, and were trying to fit in ourselves. We were totally in shock and somehow thought he was pretending to be God! We would quiz him, and hope that he would turn back into the father we had always known, but it never happened, at least not until he was institutionalized, given heavy dosages of medication, rested, and received therapy (group and one-on-one).

As adolescents we were fully aware of our dad's medical

history because during arguments our mom would usually resort to calling him "a mentally ill, epileptic fool!" And, as most all children do, seek explanations by asking her tons of questions about the superlatives she chose to use once the fight was over. She shared troubling information about daddy having seizures, "He has convulsions! His body shakes, his eyes roll back into his head, and then he sleeps for hours, and it's very scary and uncomfortable to watch."

Back then we could have benefited from some counseling and education on mental illness and epilepsy, and stronger emotional support to let us know that there were other children experiencing the same thing as we were. Our grandmother did her best, but she was limited in her explanation of his condition, and she would simply state that "he was sick and couldn't help himself." The odd thing to us was that he didn't look sick, or follow us to school like our mother did, and for that we were grateful, and didn't discuss him. But inside we couldn't help but feel confused because not one, but both of our parents were mentally ill

When daddy emerged from the hospital, he returned determined and focused, eager to put the past behind him and his life and family back together! He reunited with our mom, Geneva, who had herself completed her hospitalization in Northwestern Mental Hospital in Fort Washington, Pennsylvania.

In 1973, daddy moved our family to a spacious contemporary high-rise apartment dwelling, Kentwell Hall, in Mt. Airy, Philadelphia, Pennsylvania. It was a totally new environment for us, but I enjoyed it because we were all together once again! Lisa was beginning her first year at Martin Luther King High School, while I was completing my final year at Leeds Middle School, where I knew everyone and excelled because I was no longer in my big sister's shadow.

Unfortunately, Lisa had a difficult time adjusting to high school and often skipped school by waiting until our parents went to work and I went off to Leeds Middle School, and she would return home for the entire day pretending to be in school the whole time. She didn't hang out and play hooky with friends, indulge in drugs or even have teenage sex. I believe she was dealing with depression and issues surrounding our parents' situation, as well as the transition to high school. There was one particular incident where a few boys picked on her by throwing doughnuts at her, hitting her directly in the head, and apparently she felt intimidated by them and was afraid to discuss her fears with me or our parents. Needless to say, the situation climaxed once she ended up failing ninth grade! The following year Lisa and I were both in ninth grade together at Martin Luther King High School.

GENEVA JESSE

During this time period, my dad and mom decided to separate because "mom thought the grass was greener on the other side," hence, they fell out of love and began bickering continually. My dad who had been working for his stepfather Morris Johnson of Morris Johnson & Sons in the construction business, as well as Pete Swift's janitorial company both located in Willow Grove, Pennsylvania, was fed up with mom's adulterous behavior decided to move out! He chose to stay with one of his sisters, Amanda (Doll) or Evelyn (Daisy) in order to pay off some of his "nagging" outstanding debts.

Meanwhile, we were displaced yet again, and evicted as the locks on Sprague Street were changed because of non-payment of rent. Once again, Lisa and I ended up back in the custody of Grandma Morn, while mommy decided to move to Center City to experience life on her own terms as she lived off of unemployment benefits she gained while working one of her few jobs. She just left us to fend for ourselves. Some priority!

She stayed at some run-down, cheap motel and there she met a white man by the name of Ted Rosenstein, and quickly became pregnant by him, but she, unfortunately, was in no mental condition to care for her new baby girl, Tedefur Stone, born May 30, 1977. She asked her mother to care for her baby girl, but she declined because she had countless other responsibilities, including Lisa and me, and Tedefur became a ward of the state and went to live in a foster home. Her new foster parent was a nurse who grew very fond of baby Tedefur, and for a while mom made weekly visits to see her biracial baby girl, until the nurse decided to adopt Tedefur.

Once mom's unemployment ran out, and after Tedefur's adoption, mom came to reside with Morn, her mother, the one she had denied as her mother during her breakdown the previous year. But, that was okay, my grandmom was one forgiving woman and Geneva was her baby daughter! Lisa and I were happy as larks because we had part of our "happy family" back.

Again, daddy and mom resumed their union. They began dating one another and daddy was frequenting Peep Shows in Center City and taking her along for the ride. She tells me, "I would sit in the car as he watched and found pleasure in what he was viewing in those little peep holes he looked through, so I decided to show him what I could do, and besides there was good money in it."

Because my mom was upset that she couldn't please her husband, she decided against her morals to show him that she was just as good as the other girls he liked to watch dancing... Meanwhile, daddy attended one of the routine shows, and was startled and disgusted to find his very own wife dancing in a Peep Hole! I remember him coming to my grandmother's house announcing that, "Geneva is shaking her body downtown in a Peep Show," he said incredulously!

However, he never mentioned that he was the one who introduced the Peep Show trade to her. This was strictly out of a *Jerry Springer* show, even though it happened before Jerry.

BIRTH OF TWIN SIBLINGS
(GENEIS AND GENEVA JESSE)

Consequently, at this point, their marriage was on the rocks and Geneva met another man named William Rock, who worked at a local bakery, in Center City. Once again she became pregnant, but this time she was expecting fraternal twins (Geneis and Geneva). The twins were born July 24, 1979, and again her mental state was in question because she was delusional and talking out of her head. Again, the state of Pennsylvania was about to take them, but my grandmother decided she would help care for the adorable little twins, her grandchildren, while Geneva gets help for her mental condition.

For the next decade, mom and her twins resided with Morn on Limekiln Pike, while Lisa and I moved a few blocks away with our dad on Forrest Avenue in Philadelphia. Their marriage was ended by divorce in 1980. At first I found myself extremely embarrassed by my mom having twins by some unknown man we didn't know. I began fabricating and telling people that Geneis and Geneva were my niece and nephew because I was ashamed of my mother's behavior, getting pregnant by someone other than my dad when she was still married to him. After some time, however, I rethought my lies and began telling the truth about my little brother and sister because, after all, it wasn't their fault they existed, and I was growing to love my sweet little babies.

When Geneis and Geneva were born, Lisa and I were nineteen and eighteen years old respectively, and just beginning to make our own paths in life, adjusting to working, getting married and starting families. The twins were very lovable babies, and even though our fathers may have been different, they resemble us. Geneis, our only brother, has attributes and features similar to mine, he is pensive and on the reserved side and his complexion is light, while Geneva resembles Lisa, heavy-set, brown-skinned and very bubbly and sociable. In school Geneis flourished, while Geneva had learning challenges early on.

GENEVA JESSE (SISTER)

Geneva is a very sweet and helpful young lady. Unfortunately, she repeated first, second, and third grade twice at Daniel E. Carnell and Pennypacker Elementary Schools, indicating learning difficulties, and we began recognizing that she was having serious problems.

Amazingly, she made it to high school where she

attended Martin Luther King (MLK) high and even made the honor roll for the very first time.

When she was sixteen years old, she began hallucinating and complaining of "seeing an imaginary white lady who she feared was following her and instructing her to harm herself." We knew instantly that she was exhibiting mental illness, and that she was behaving the exact same way our mother had years prior, except that our mother who was normally mild-mannered would get agitated and yell expletives at the television professing to be white. She was hospitalized a number of times and placed on many different types of medication for schizophrenia. I remember she developed a phobia about chicken; she wouldn't eat it because she thought it was poison. She was transferred to Greentree Upper School in the ninth grade and graduated in 2000. At Greentree she flourished! She met a lot of friends, and even took a liking to a young man named Steven Lee who became her first boyfriend.

She is currently residing in Brian's House located in West Chester which helps children and adults with mental retardation, autism spectrum disorders and other developmental disabilities. She's lived there now for over seven years, and it has taken the strain of taking her back and forth to the hospital off my mother. In addition, mom doesn't have to monitor her medication regimen or her extracurricular activities. Brian's House has been a great resource and excellent place for Geneva to live because they help her with her individual needs. They monitor her progress, her interactions with others, recreational activities including plenty of community events, movies, shows, trips to the mall, insure that she makes her doctor appointments, and transports her to my home for weekend visits. She is currently taking Cloziril to control her psychotic behavior and Zoloft for depression.

Schizophrenia is a chronic, severe, and disabling brain disease. As defined by Web MD, people with schizophrenia often suffer terrifying symptoms such as hearing internal voices not heard by others, or believing that other people are reading their minds, controlling their thoughts, or plotting to harm them.

These symptoms may leave them fearful and withdrawn. Their speech and behavior can be so disorganized that they may be incomprehensible or frightening to others. Available treatments can relieve many symptoms, but most people with schizophrenia continue to suffer some symptoms throughout their lives; it has been estimated that no more than one in five individuals recovers completely.

Because my mom developed her illness when she and my dad were separated and she couldn't provide for us suggests to me that the onset of her illness was partially brought on because of anxiety. I believe that because mom couldn't take care of us financially because of her lack of a particular skill, and because of her isolating herself, even though she has lots of family, she allowed her pride to prevent her from reaching out.

My mom has suffered through countless bouts of schizophrenia in her lifetime, but began worshipping at Mt. Airy Church of God and has not had a breakdown in over twenty plus years, thank God, and has joined me in joining Enon Tabernacle Baptist Church in Philadelphia, Pennsylvania.

GENEIS JESSE

Geneis is a handsome and very pensive young man. He

reminds me of myself when I was younger, not much for small talk, but full of observation. He graduated from Martin Luther King High School, and attended Lincoln University for over a year, but began having difficulties after Lisa passed away.

He served eight years in the United States Navy where he was a Machinist Mate. Geneis is currently residing in Virginia with his wife, Cynthia, of five years. They recently purchased their first home, a lovely two bedroom condominium. Presently, Geneis is working in the Boiler Operations field and recently completed his CFC Certification in Heating, Ventilation, Air-Conditioning and Refrigeration (HVACR), and is pursuing a career with the United States Federal Government.

DARKNESS

FEAR   PAIN

   CONFUSION

SADNESS
         LOST

SECRETS

                    QUIET

ANGER

          HIDING

MARIO, MY KNIGHT
IN SHINING ARMOR

CHAPTER V

MARIO, THE GOOD, THE BAD, THE UGLY (1973)

At the age of thirteen, just a year after I started menstruating, my life, and more especially boys, meant very little to me because I considered myself a diehard tomboy (nondescript light-skinned, 117 lbs., with short, corn-rowed braids), until I met him! Mario Corvette Bosman! He and I were almost the same height, as long as I didn't wear heels, but in those days sneakers were my standard foot attire. He was a compact five feet four inches tall, kind of short for a man by society's standards, but in my eyes he appeared to be my knight in shining armor and stood seven feet twelve inches!

Initially, because he was three years older than I was I felt a little intimidated by him because I imagined that he would be either too wise or too experienced (fast) for me, but he soon dispelled my personal myths and satisfied my uneasiness with his childlike charm. He had a strong muscular build with huge bulging arms and a rock hard six-pack, a stark contrast from the boys who had yet to go through puberty in my seventh grade class at Morris E. Leeds Middle School on Mt. Pleasant and Thouron Avenues in the Mount Airy section of Philadelphia, Pennsylvania.

Mario was totally unlike other boys I knew. He was fine! He reminded me of Marlon Jackson of the infamous Jackson 5 clan, and even wore his hair very similar small-sized afro. He was light-skinned, with big luscious lips, which could have themselves been an ad for botox injections, except in those days having large lips was a little shameful. His piercing chocolate brown eyes seemed to see right through me and connect to my very essence.

Mario was one of five brothers, Artavious (Arty), Cecil, Angelo and Quinton (Quincy), and they were very popular among all the local girls, sort of like the neighborhood Jackson 5, New Edition or Boys to Men singing groups. They were all very good looking and shared those signature luscious lips, wore nothing but the finest leather jackets, had their own family band with each of them playing an instrument, and three of them were allegedly in the neighborhood Uptown Valley gang, a spin-off of the original North Philly Valley gang, and the heartthrobs of many.

Arty was the oldest and happened to be albino. He played the bass guitar and was away at the Variety Club Camp all summer long because he was a camp counselor. Quincy was the youngest and attended Roman Catholic High School where he played basketball, which kept him extremely busy. Usually he was either at practice or participating in one of their games. That left Mario, who played drums and the twins, Cecil and Angelo playing saxophone and the guitar respectively. Their mother, Mary Elaine Bosman, a wonderfully kind and shapely woman, was a private-duty nurse who worked the graveyard shift, sought a better life for her boys and sent them to St. Theresa's Catholic School at Upsal and Ardleigh. However, the twins kept bringing toys to school, and she was advised to separate them so they could establish their own identities, which brings us to the reason Cecil attended Leeds Middle School, where he was so popular amongst many of the girls, Lisa being one! As latch-key kids, they were instructed to "go straight home, complete their homework, change clothes, and wait for their mom to arrive from work."

One particularly sunny day, we (Lisa, Putt, Thomasina Martina and I) decided to follow Cecil home. We rang the doorbell and asked for Cecil and were ushered into the living room by Cecil himself. Seeking mischief, the four of us piled on the soft fluffy sofa and waited. Angelo, Cecil and Mario were quietly sitting on the ascending sky blue carpeted stairwell, peering through the wrought iron railing observing their waiting prey. Someone suggested we play a game called "Catch a Girl, Kiss a Girl," and suddenly, the lights went out and we anxiously waited to be kissed before the lights went back on.

I sat there frozen with delight for what seemed like an eternity waiting, hoping that someone would find me and help me discover what it would be like to be a girl, and not the tomboy everyone perceived me to be, and then all of a sudden it happened! I felt total sweetness wrapped up in warm luscious marshmellowy lips all over my dry mouth. I could feel my heart pounding, thump, thump, thump, and butterflies dancing and birds chirping inside my head.

I attempted to act like a lady and contain myself on the outside, but inside I was bursting with delight! I wondered what the other girls were doing. And then I just let myself feel and went with the flow of the moment, rationalizing that it was dark and no one could see what was happening to me inside. Inside I was passionate, free and uninhibited and Mario was unlocking something deep within me, and I couldn't help but part my lips and search for the treasure between his teeth, licking his gums, finding his tongue... and then the lights went on! Flooded with emotion and dizzy with intoxication us school girls went home giggling with joy and rehashing the details of our first kiss! From that day forward, I replayed that kiss over and over again in my head, and fantasized about the day that my first kiss would be repeated. Oh yes, it would be repeated. It was our destiny!

Each day I dressed with the intention of hopefully running in to Mario and matching up that kiss. I daydreamed day and night, and didn't have to wait until I went to sleep at night because I discovered I could visualize our kiss any time of the day when I was happy or sad. I couldn't help but compare myself to Cinderella because I loved that fairytale growing up, and up until this point I had never experienced anything that would even remotely come near the experience of being found by my prince. In a moment I went from being a tomboy to becoming a young woman with desire for that young man who steered deep emotion within me. It was a wonderful story and I truly felt beautiful. Life at home was unbearable with both parents having mental breakdowns and losing our home in a Sheriff's (foreclosure) sale, but I escaped often to my daydreams (light sleeps) of that kiss and marrying my prince. I always had my eyes open for

Mario, especially hoping to see him on Vernon Road. He started coming up to Leeds, hopefully looking for me, but it appeared more like Leeds was becoming the hang-out for the Valley gang. Even though we both seemed to enjoy that kiss, we didn't have much else in common.

Unfortunately, I wasn't the only girl who had eyes for Mario. A mixed girl, small in stature, sort of Spanish-looking with long beautifully naturally straight black hair, named Carmen Vest was rumored to be Mario's new Valley girl. I didn't think she was that attractive, but she hung out in their circle. At that time it was traditional for guys to have gang girls. While Carmen was throwing herself at Mario I knew that he had to be obliging. Mario was trying to reconnect with me, but I wanted to be his one and only! Mario was good at boxing and became the Young-Boy Runner. The gang met at Edmonds Elementary School, where we passed by on our way home from school, where they drank Thunderbird, Mad Dog, 20–20 and cheap wine that got them high, catching the rams, and testing one another on their manhood by slap boxing and trying to find rank status in the gang.

We somehow lost touch after our parents lost our home on Temple Road and we went to live with our grandmother on Limekiln Pike, and Mario and his brothers were sent away to a boarding school, Downingtown Industrial School for Boys and Girls, to circumvent the gang activity, but a friend we both knew who was in this reform school with Mario shared that Mario was still carrying the torch for me, and asked me to write him because he was lonely, and I began writing, and he in turn wrote and our letters turned from friendship to passion. A year later after that first kiss it was destined to happen. Mario Corvette Bosman and I became inseparable after that fateful Halloween night in October 1975 when we awkwardly made love as teenagers in my cramped small twin bed in our third floor apartment at Kentwell Hall on Sprague Street after my parents left to attend Halloween festivities at the home of friends in Willingboro, New Jersey. Lisa, who was my official escort when we were younger, wasn't that far away at Mario's grandmother's house with his brothers waiting for me and Mario to return from around the corner.

Soon after that, Mario gave me some type of bubblegum ring to signify that we were indeed united and now shared his title for our togetherness "pure love."

While Mario was away at school, our "pure love" grew stronger, and I learned to pen my feelings in letters to the young man I hoped would be my husband and in my life forever. When he would come home from school we were inseparable.

After Mario graduated from high school he decided to join the United States Army in 1976, and I, being three years younger than he (fifteen years old), would only fantasize about being his wife and traveling the world with him. By this time my letter writing skills were getting perfected as I wrote to him every day expressing my undying love for him. He, in turn, wrote letters whenever he could.

When he graduated from Boot Camp in Fort Dix, New Jersey, Lisa and I accompanied his sweet mother and his stepfather William Hughes to the ceremony. When he was stationed close to home in Fayetteville, North Carolina, Mario came home to see his sweetheart every weekend he was permitted.

I remember Mario taught me how to drive in his tiny red Chevrolet Chevette, leaving his car with me even before I received my learner's permit. That was one thing about him, he believed in me, even before I believed in myself.

This was an extremely delicate time at home for me, because my home life was in turmoil with both of my parents experiencing mental breakdowns, and me turning to Mario for comfort and support.

HAIR LOSS (ALOPECIA)

For some unknown reason my hair began to fall out. I rationalized that I lost my hair because beauticians applied chemical (perm) relaxers that were too strong for my hair type, including the first relaxer being administered by my very own mother, who knew not what she was doing, or perhaps the stress of life. Who knew? Whatever the cause, my hair became very fragile, thinned out and eventually I couldn't cover up the missing spots! I had bald patches all over my head, and I was going through puberty, my precious teen years, but I still had to attend school, if I planned on graduating as planned and creating my dream life with my pure love Mario.

I had to think quickly because school didn't stop just because my hair was missing. Using my ingenuity, I decided to purchase scarves in all types of colors to match my every outfit, and fortunately my solution to my dilemma worked because this was during the era in the 1970's when many young people were professing to be Muslims and dressing accordingly with all types of hair garments and wraps to cover their hair, and most people just assumed I was either Muslim or setting my own style. Fortunately, for me, Mario was caring and understanding of everything! He would take my scarves off my balding head and massage it gently and even involved his mother, Mrs. Bosman, in on helping me to take care of my hair. Once it started growing back, she would straighten and curl my hair the old-fashioned way, using a straightening comb, and giving my hair a glistening effect, Mario termed "candy curls."

Because of my low self-esteem and Mario's popularity I rationalized, I questioned Mario's faithfulness all the time. I often heard rumors of him cheating with several girls, including Cherry Helago, Carmen Vest, and someone named Kimmy.

This was during the time my parents were estranged from one another and we were residing with our Grandmother Morn on Limekiln Pike and my dad, William Jesse, made weekly visits to see me and Lisa. He would bring us allowances and gifts and Lisa seemed happy, but I was always crying and asking for help to cure my baldness! My daddy always tried hard to please us girls, and seemed to take it to heart if he couldn't change a situation. He was determined to help boost my self-concept and really extended himself by locating a hair clinic/doctor in Center City called Frommes Hair Research and decided to take me there.

He was the best dad ever! Every weekend, preferably on Saturday, we made the trek to Frommes Hair Research, and for the first time in a long time, I was excited because hopefully before long I would have my hair back, and maybe it would come back thicker and healthier than Lisa's, and I could be a normal teenager again and attend school without something wrapped on my head.

I was diagnosed with alopecia, defined simply by Webster's New World College Dictionary, Fourth Edition, as "baldness or loss of hair." Each Saturday I would see their physician and an assistant who would massage my scalp with some different colored hair tonic/concoction in small circular motions to help stimulate the hair follicles to encourage my bald scalp to begin re-growth, and then I would sit under a heat lamp for a specified time period. The ritual was welcoming for me because I was going through puberty, and my fragile ego was in need of repair. The assistant would exclaim, "Oh, I see some new hair coming in." In addition, the Frommes technicians suggested I keep the little bit of hair on my head as loose and stress-free as possible, and suggested I not attempt to straighten or braid my fragile strands.

Frommes was extremely costly for my dad who ended up spending excessive sums of cash on varied solutions for re-growth of hair, as the clinic supposedly sold only the highest quality of tonics. Each tonic was uniquely colored and designed to invigorate the hair follicles in one way or another. One was supposed to do this and another was supposed to do that, but we were beginning to feel like daddy was getting milked because on sight it appeared like nothing was occurring. The longer we continued making the treks to the clinic, the more disillusioned I became because I really didn't notice any hair growing in the bald patches, and my poor dad had to spend increasingly more money.

Eventually, I stopped believing in Frommes and the hair products, and decided to give my dad a break. We stopped making those expensive trips, and I began going to my cousin Robin's Hair Salon in Jenkintown to have my hair washed and curled the old-fashioned way. Thus, fortunately, by the time I graduated from high school, my hair had grown in enough so that I could wear it to my prom.

BIRTH CONTROL

At some point, Lisa and I went to the free Clinic in Germantown at the suggestion of Tine. Lisa objected to taking birth control pills because she wasn't sexually active, but I accepted readily. During this time, Mario went away into the Army and was scheduled to serve overseas in Germany for a year, he suggested that I "save myself for him," and because I loved him with all my heart, I stopped taking my prescribed birth control pills.

However, once Mario left for Germany, I, along with Lisa and some friends used to hang out every weekend at the "Old Wagner's Ballroom" and dance the night away. Concurrently, daddy was back to dreaming of ways to make money. He devised a plan to sponsor dances at the Old Wagner's Ballroom and use his daughters' (Lisa and Bridget Jesse) "The Jesse girls" as a marketing strategy to draw our friends and other teenagers because we had recently held a dynamite graduation party at Calico Kitchen, he thought he'd make a profit!

UNEXPECTED PREGNANCY

It was during this time frame, while Mario was serving in Germany, that I became physically attracted to a guy named Eugene, just because he could dance and looked sexy in his fitted shirt. I didn't even know much about him. What I did know was that he lived in the poorest neighborhood in Philly and resided in the Richard Allen Projects and I never even intentioned to peer inside, he reeked of a sour smell in his clothing, sort-of like perspiration and cologne mixed in with soiled laundry. But that didn't stop me from engaging with him in a temporary thrill.

Some time after one of the weekend parties Lisa and I hosted, I took Eugene home with me at 3:00 a.m. to my grandmother's house because I knew that everyone in the household would be fast asleep, including my Aunt who was asleep just yards away on the living room couch.

A few months passed by and I remember fainting, I thought that it was because it was summer and I was extremely overheated, but here it was, months had passed by and I missed my period a few times, and when I went to my physician he seemed to know right away, with the teenage pregnancy epidemic being high in the city of Philadelphia, to perform a simple urine exam test to find out what he already suspected, that I was a few months … Pregnant!

What a disaster! Ssh, please don't tell, I instructed my family, especially my sometimes "big mouth" bribing sister, Lisa. If Mario found out my Cinderella fantasy life was over! At only fifteen years old, I was keenly aware that I must make a decision!

I discussed my dire circumstances with my dad, and even though he yelled and scolded me, his chastisement meant very little compared to the thought of losing the man of my dreams to a bum that I allowed to penetrate, even if he didn't put it all the way in, me on a warm summer's night in July and who never really meant anything to me.

FIRST ABORTION

My dad decided to help me find a way to terminate my pregnancy before Mario found out and it would be too late. I received some counseling about whether or not to terminate the pregnancy, but, at the time, the decision for me was a no-brainer, and that's exactly what I did! Obviously, I made the wrong decision. "Children are a gift from the Lord; they are a reward from him" (Psalm 127:3).

Academically, I was an honor student, inducted into the National Honor Society, and assisted the school as a nurse's aid. My self-esteem was extremely low, and because of my family situation and hair loss, I was vulnerable! Loving Mario gave me an emotional outlet and a purpose. I loved him sincerely, with my full heart. Even though he gave me a bubblegum ring to signify our relationship, I often heard tales of his infidelity, or whispers about him spending time with other girls. But he always denied any unfaithfulness, and I pretended to believe him, when I didn't trust him as far as I could see him because something inside me, perhaps my knowing intuition, didn't believe him. He said he only loved me and when he was there he demonstrated this. We were together as much as possible and made pure love often. I stayed with him because I couldn't get enough of his love. His love was intoxicating, even if, I only trusted him as far as I could see.

The rumor mill was always spitting out truths about him with Carmen, Sherry or Kimmy, but that didn't stop me from loving the ground he walked on! Every time he returned to the Army, I cried like an overgrown infant losing her bottle, until I began releasing my emotions into the love letters I poured my heart and soul in as I wrote Mario almost daily. I immersed myself into my school work when he was away, wrote him daily, and ended up ranking twenty-one out of approximately 500 graduating seniors. But then that was a city school (Martin Luther King) and at that time, not much was required of students, except that we attend school, and this was during the time when students were allowed to design our own curricular and pick projects. For example, if you were required to take English, students could choose projects he/she enjoyed as opposed to assignments that would challenge and strengthen him/her and help him learn. Invariably I always chose reading novels and completing book reports because of my passion for reading, but I don't agree with the method of teaching. Lisa and I majored in business/academic courses. We enrolled in advanced typing and advanced shorthand, and did internships at area businesses. I couldn't wait to graduate because my focus was on marrying Mario. I graduated a year ahead of time by attending evening school where I took Bookkeeping 101 to make up for the graduation requirements. Unfortunately, after I graduated I was only seventeen years old, inexperienced, and couldn't find a job! In essence, I hurried up, just to have to wait!

Lisa and I considered becoming court stenographers, but ended up attending the Philadelphia School of Office Training (PSOT) where we majored in Legal Secretarial Science, after we were denied acceptance to any of the local colleges we applied to because we were lousy test takers, and apparently we bombed on our entrance exams and/or we applied too late. We attempted to attend Pierce Junior College for court stenography, but were declined because we did not meet their requirements as well, but we never gave up, and finally we were accepted at PSOT, where we excelled. We were considered the shining stars and considered most likely to obtain employment in our field once we graduated!

After struggling for eighteen months at PSOT, it was finally over and time for us to seek employment. Lisa received a position as a Legal Secretary, while I was hired on December 17, 1979, as a Junior Clerk with stenography skills. Although it was not a legal secretarial position, it was ideal for me because the legal profession was much too abstruse; having to dot i's and cross t's was a little to strict for me. I was ecstatic when I was hired by Mr. Walter Senek, a vice president of a major utility where I met one of my new best friends, Doris Graham.

At this local utility I envisioned myself flourishing because there were countless individuals achieving the success I so desired, and they were close enough for what they knew to influence my decisions. I worked directly in the midst of several such individuals, either with college educations/pursuing advanced degrees, Jacqueline Simms, Bernadette Gant-Jones, and Edward Graham (deceased), and they inspired me to continue my education. In 1981 I applied and was accepted to LaSalle University (LSU). However, after taking the entrance exam, LSU determined that I was deficient in Math, and required I take a remedial course to strengthen my skills. I wasn't discouraged! I thought, "If the only thing that's keeping me from a college education is a course, I would gladly pay the non-refundable fee to take it, and move on my way to realizing my dream!

CHAPTER VI

MARRIAGE TO MARIO
(1981)

I finally got my wish and convinced Mario Corvette Bosman to marry me. "Be careful what you ask for, you just might get it." It was during my favorite season of the year, fall, when the earth tone colors are so vibrant, October 17, 1981, a few days before my twentieth birthday. Our nuptials were performed by Mario's maternal grandfather, the late Rev. Victor Carson, in a delightfully wholesome ceremony of close knit family and friends. However, only one person was glaringly missing from the bridal party, the mother-of-the-bride, my dear mother, Geneva Jesse! Unfortunately, mom was MIA because she was in the midst of having one of her episodes, and quite frankly, secretly I was hoping she wasn't aware of the site of the wedding because she could show up in her delusional mental state and ruin our festivities.

Our wedding took place at Cedar Park Presbyterian Church. We didn't belong to the church, nor were we members of any church, at the time. We decided on the location because of the spectacular visibility, and paid for the use of their facilities. It was probably an omen because I cried from the moment I walked down the aisle, with my nervous father stepping on my train, after having his afro blown-out at the beauty parlor by cousin, Robin (Nay-Nay) Huff. His hair resembled that of a scared porcupine. No kidding.

It was a large bridal party which consisted of six bridesmaids and six groomsmen. Because of the season, my color scheme was deeper hues - burgundy and gray, the young ladies wore burgundy evening gowns with little pillbox hats consisting of an attached tiny little veil, and the young men wore sharp charcoal gray tuxedos. Of course, my sister Lisa was my maid of honor, and she was radiant in her pink gown as she strolled down the aisle five months pregnant carrying her beloved only child, Terrance Jesse.

The other bridesmaids consisted of Tine Stone and twin cousins Jacqueline (Jackie) Huff and Gwendolyn (Gwennie) Basketbill, and best friends, Putt Jenkins and Doris Graham. Mario's groomsmen consisted of all his brothers, Artavious, twins Cecil and Angelo, Quinton, his uncle Bobby Carson, and cousin Demetrious (Mecco) Baxter, and boy did I dislike Mecco. Mecco was Mario's favorite cousin, and to top it off they shared the same birth date and were "partners in crime." The flower girls were Yarnell Huff, Sharon Carson and Kimberly Brown, and the ring bearer was Tine's son, Raheem Abdullah.

The day was surreal, and I could barely contain myself, the man I loved was truly going to be mine! After countless arguments regarding other women claiming they had been with him, and his subsequent denials, and excuses for why he wasn't ready to get married, "he didn't have enough money," "he didn't have a house," "he didn't have a good enough job," etc. We purchased our very first home a few doors away from my grandmother's home on Limekiln Pike in August 1981, and Mario married me and I mistakenly thought that his philandering would end! Incorrect! No such luck, but that was the beginning of the nightmare continuing in my romance to the guy of my dreams!

INFIDELITY AND WE WERE JUST MARRIED

We honeymooned in Disney World in Florida, and I stayed on a marital high at least until we returned home, and the truth began to unravel. I went over to Angelo (Mario's brother) and Jackie's house looking for Mario, and what I discovered was the beginning of the nightmare—Kelly Breezeway with my husband Mario! Of course, he denied that they were together, and claimed to be "only friends," but then after that evening Kelly became a flea that just wouldn't go away! From the time we were married in 1981 until I finally divorced him in 1990, not a year went by that Kelly and Mario didn't carry on their affair.

There may have been other girls, but not to my knowledge. Well, there was one other documented infidelity that I was aware of before we wed, and this should have given me a clue of his character then, that still small voice inside me tried to forewarn me. Some girl named Helen was claiming that Mario fathered her infant son, Dwayne, and Helen took him to court, where the DNA stated that there was an 80% chance that Mario was the father of baby Dwayne. And, with that ruling, his wages were attached! That was an embarrassing situation because although Mario had warned me of his potential fatherhood position after being made aware of the situation by Helen before we married, we both worked at the same employer, and once his wages were attached, everyone in the Treasury Department knew. Great way to begin our marriage!

    Kelly made herself a royal pain in the neck every chance she could get! Every time it looked like things were improving between us, I would get a phone call reminding me she was there and that she would never quit, ever, and that any time he wasn't with me, he was with her. She staked out my house and waited for me to leave to be with my husband. I didn't feel the bliss I thought a newlywed should be experiencing. When that 1987 popular movie *Fatal Attraction*, in which Michael Douglas had an affair with Glenn Close and she wouldn't let their romance die, came out, I thought the script was stolen from my life because that was the first time I ever saw the depth of how bizarre a woman scorned could go, and it illustrated the emotional torture experienced by his wife (Anne Archer and me). I didn't feel safe! I did all I could to block out the affair, pretending it did not exist, to fist-fighting and challenging her mentally.

    I even tried befriending her. I figured I'd kill her with as much kindness as I could since they were claiming to be "only friends."

    Thinking back, sometimes when Mario was at home, the telephone would ring non-stop, and I would be afraid to answer it because that little evil, malicious witch would be so bold and brazen to ask to speak to my husband, "is Mario home?"

    "No, yeah, please stop calling here, I would plead. Mario's my husband and no you can't speak to him. Please don't call here again!" Click! She continued to call so much so that

I would sometimes just unplug the phone! I tried changing our number, but then somehow, some way she would get our number once again, and repeatedly I was puzzled. I quizzed Mario on "how she continued to obtain our number?" To which he'd reply, "I don't know."

On one occasion Mario came home very troubled as he shared with me that Kelly thought she was pregnant. To which I replied, "What? Well, if she is, she planned it that way trying to trap you into a relationship with her," I reasoned "Do you want her to have it?"

"No," he replied, "but she says she's going to keep it," he replied meekly."

"Well, if she is pregnant, and you don't want her to have it, I'm not giving you to her. Let's invite her over and talk to her civilly like grown-ups handling a difficult situation, since we were twenty and twenty-three respectively."

That meeting was a total disaster because she didn't look pregnant to me, but I did get a chance to size up my competition!

"What does she have that I don't have, I thought?" She was brown-skinned and very skinny. She didn't look special to me at all! She sort of looked like a tomboy with her big feet, housed in high-top converse boy sneakers. Her hair looked half combed and she had large teeth that overlapped, and of course, she had a devious, conniving mind she used to size me up and create trouble.

I pretended to not be affected when she barked "I look better than you!" Or "Yuck, she would squeal, you can't keep your man, or, he was with me, and is with me anytime he isn't with you!" But, I did learn that she was a liar, and not pregnant at all, just attempting to stir the pot of trouble.

Sometimes I would eavesdrop on the telephone and

overhear Mario talking to Kelly, and, I would be livid! "How on earth can you continue to talk to that girl when it hurts me so deeply," I would say?

To which he'd reply, "She's just my friend, Bridget." She's in some sort of trouble. Her mom kicked her out of the house, or she needs my help, etc." I couldn't understand this so-called relationship with me being his wife! I definitely had a difficult time coping with this so-called friendship situation. My already very fragile self-esteem took a deeper plunge, but I was determined to hold on to my man! I realized I was playing a dangerous game with a cunning individual, but I didn't want my marriage to fail when it had just begun.

She pretended to just be his friend, and sometimes tried worming her way into our marriage whenever Mario would reject her. On the nights when he didn't return home, I would cry myself to sleep, only to be greeted by him returning in the morning with passion marks on his neck, smacking me dead in my face as outright disregard for my feelings. I came to realize he didn't respect me! I thought I was losing my mind because he continually lied to my face about his whereabouts and his feelings for this outsider, but I saw and felt with my very own eyes. I was at a crossroads too early in my marriage for it to end with me conceding loss to this girl who, I rationalized, wanted what I had, and was trying her best to break us up. And what did I do? I decided to have his child to do one or two, 1. Unite us as a couple or to 2. Commemorate our marriage after it was over.

Several months later, I was carrying his child, and I thought "if this doesn't put an end to Mario's unfaithfulness, nothing would."

During May 1985 I went on maternity leave from my job

where I was now secretary to the manager of Affirmative Action at the utility I was working at and I hoped the infidelity would end because I was now having his son! We knew we were having a baby boy because of the ultra-sound. But, let's just say for the record, just because I got pregnant didn't change the situation one bit, or, if anything, it seemed to escalate and get worse! He was the same cheater he was before I got pregnant.

It was an early Monday morning and we were sleeping blissfully late because of the beautiful surprise baby showers we had been given over the weekend by our family, friends, and coworkers and normally I would be at work, but I was now at home on an early maternity leave from work because I was retaining fluid around my ankles and needed to stay off my feet, and Mario was also at home because it was his regularly scheduled day off because he worked weekends, and had Mondays off. I felt so happy and excited because of all the love and wonderful gifts we had been given. We had recently painted the baby's room white and decorated it with Disney characters, reminding us of that special honeymoon we had been given by my father four years back, and now we were having our first child! Wow!

I'm awakened by someone ringing the doorbell. Ring, ring, ring. I answered the door. Oh no! My world comes crashing down around me. Kelly Breezeway is there looking just as stunned as I am to see her! "Is Mario home," she questions?

"Don't you have any respect or decency?" Before she could answer, I yell for Mario to come see about this brazenfaced woman! As he dresses to escort her away from the house, I cry, question, and demand explanations! I emphatically suggest he deal with the situation, but my head is spinning out of control because I truthfully don't know how to deal with this issue because it is now obvious to me that she has been secretly spending time at my house with my husband on Mondays, his scheduled day off work!

During the next few weeks to come, as if out of some sort of horror picture, I am constantly reminded of the fact that Kelly has been present in my home on more than one occasion. Under the teddy bear, on the walls, on my pillow, and in my car, the girl had engraved her name somewhere for me to notice. This girl was some nut case! She was Mario's mistress, flaunting herself shamelessly for all to see.

(1985) BIRTH OF MY FIRST SON, MARIO BRIT BOSMAN

On June 30, 1985, Mario Brit Bosman, weighing seven pounds, five ounces, was born. I chose to name our baby after his father. I was so exhausted and spent, but happy because Mario Corvette was there supporting me during natural childbirth and to welcome our baby into the world and I sincerely hoped life would improve from there.

Unfortunately, my sister, Lisa, who wasn't one to hold her tongue, was so disgusted with his behavior after Mario Brit's birth while I was still in the hospital she just had to tell me what was on her mind because she was seething with contempt for the way he was disrespecting me!

She said, "Bridget, Mario was riding around in your car with the tee tops down with that girl, Kelly Breezeway, and had the nerve to pass me by as I stood on the corner waiting for the bus to bring me to the hospital."

I was twenty-four years old and completely drained after birthing Mario Brit with no pain medication, I had been suffering with Mario's constant philandering since I married him four years prior, and there was absolutely nothing I could do about this situation now because I couldn't even stop him from seeing her before I had my baby. I tried breastfeeding baby Mario, but developed an infection and a temperature which didn't allow me to nurse him. I kept my emotions pretty bottled up before I had Mario, but at this point I developed a bad case of the blues, and I cried a lot. I was diagnosed with postpartum depression, and fortunately Mario's mother was a nurse and she became our private-duty nurse as well.

Their romance blossomed to the point Mario wouldn't come home on nights when he had money or got paid. In the beginning when he would disappear I would be so worried, pacing the floor all night, crying, passively watching television and hoping he'd call or come in the door any minute, but he wouldn't show up until the next day when the sun came up. I would interrogate him, curse him out, plead with him, and beg him to stay with me, and even got on my knees to and plead several times. On a few of those occasions, he would return home and sink into the bathtub to relax, but then I would notice passion marks on his neck, indicating to me that Kelly had more than likely been sucking on him, and wanted me to be aware of her signature imprint, I knew the girl was a vampire with those big teeth she had! And, sure enough as day, she would call and give me a blow-by-blow description of their time together.

Why was I torturing myself? This man obviously had zero respect for me!

I would painfully ask through tears of humiliation and pain," Are you in love with her? Do you want her or me?"

To which he would always answer, "You. I love you,

Bridget, with all my heart and I keep telling her that I'm never going to leave you, and to leave me and you alone, but she won't."

Reflecting back when we first married and moved to Limekiln Pike, Kelly called my father's house on Forrest Avenue and had the audacity to call and ask my sister Lisa, "Can I speak to Mario?"

To which, Lisa replied, "Girl, Mario is married, and he doesn't live here anymore! Don't call here again." Kelly said something smart to Lisa, and Lisa suggested that she come there and say it to her face. Needless to say, a few minutes later, Kelly showed up at my dad's house, and Lisa and Kelly proceeded to fist-fight. Lisa telephoned us and gave Mario a piece of her mind! The climate was pretty intense, and now my secret was out! I was extremely embarrassed because I had been trying to pretend to be happy. Here I am married, had that expensive wedding which I was now in debt over and my spouse is cheating with this heifer and now everyone is aware!

Being truthful with myself, it had escalated to the point I didn't even feel safe or comfortable in my own home because there were signs and evidence of Mario bringing Kelly there. One night after I had Mario Brit, I went to bed, and awoke to my husband missing again, and this was beginning to be a pattern. When I got up to look for him in the house, I overheard a commotion downstairs, and I went to see what was going on, and there is Mario and Kelly tussling in my living room. I look on in disbelief as I cradle Lil Mario in my arms ever so tight, like I'm having an out-of-body experience, as if in a dream state. This is surreal. They both glance at us out of the corner of their eyes.

"What is this girl doing in my house, when I'm supposed to be asleep upstairs?

"Hit her, Bridget," Mario yelled out, as he scrambled to get his footing. "Call the police." Anxiously, I called 911 and the police officers arrived a few minutes later. "Officer, this girl is trespassing in my house," I announced boldly.

"Well, there are no signs of forced entry, apparently she was let in."

I explained the situation to the police officers and asked what would have happened to me had I hit her as Mario suggested, and their reply was that she could turn around and sue me because she didn't force her way into our home. I'm realizing more and more that this girl is a fatal attraction, but Mario definitely has some fault in this situation as well!

Another bizarre incident occurred just a few months later. Mario and I retired to bed at the same time, but as soon as I went to sleep, he disappeared and this time took my car! He stayed away from home a few days, and although I was embarrassed, I needed my car to get to work, so I enlisted the support of Putt, to drive me to find my car because I had an idea of where my car could be. I thought about a place he had driven me one day to pick up a package. I was no dummy, and I was aware of what the news had been saying about this particular part of town, and bingo, we locate my red Chevy Camaro in North Philadelphia around ninth and Butler, a well-known drug-infested neighborhood, and in it we find Mario and Kelly sprawled out on the front passenger seat like they belonged in my car. "Get out," I exclaimed, and snatched my keys from a docile non-resistant Mario as he profusely apologized.

My self-esteem was so crushed that I tolerated the abuse,

and turned around and planned to have his child anyway because, at that time, I reasoned, Mario was the love of my life, and I might never find anyone else to love me the way I loved him! I also hoped it would repair our marriage, but the unfaithfulness only escalated.

After that incident, I still hadn't figured out what sort of hold Kelly had over Mario, but then Mario decided to come clean, and tell the truth, He began to bare all as he disclosed that he and Kelly did drugs together and she oftentimes supplied him! It made sense! I didn't indulge in drugs, he kept that from me, and I knew Mario smoked joint on occasion, and it became crystal clear because now I was hearing talks of crack cocaine use by Mario!

DADDY'S SECOND MARRIAGE

Just when my honeymoon was ending, my dad remarried and his honeymoon was beginning. A month after I gave birth to Mario Brit on July 23, 1985, my dad exchanged wedding vows with my stepmother. She had two sons that were many years younger than me and Lisa. They enjoyed blending us all together over birthdays and holidays, and for the most part we looked forward to our bonding times together. The rituals they established were a much needed change in our family. However, life continued to worsen at home between me and Mario.

CHAPTER VII

HOW DO I DEAL WITH A SPOUSE ADDICTED TO DRUGS?

(1989)

Wow, what a nightmare this was! I was so confused, but kind of relieved in a way. I theorized that it was the drugs, not Kelly after all. It got to the point where Mario was messing up both at home and at work. At home our finances went haywire! Our joint bank account had zero funds and the mortgage was overdue. I had to devise a way to make sure the mortgage was paid because I didn't want to lose our home the way my parents lost their home to a dreadful sheriff's sale many years back. Mario was a good-hearted person, and he didn't want us to lose our home either, and he seemed helpless in a sense and wanted to cooperate once he was sober or down off the drugs. He set up payroll deduction to go straight to my bank account, and left a minimal amount of money, just enough to survive weekly.

Unfortunately, his other bills suffered, he totaled his car, and stole things around the house. Many times he went on his drug binges, and begged and pleaded for me to lend/give him money, and, I usually tried to stick to my guns and refusing. For the most part, I began sleeping with my money and jewelry of value under my pillow. I remember my bicycle disappeared, in a phony break-in where small valuables were stolen, and to this day I believe Mario had his hand in it. In addition, his mom was great at supplying him with money so many times he badgered her for the money he needed to fund his bad habits

At work he was missing time, acting bizarrely and as a result had to submit to a drug (urine) test, which he failed miserably. In order to keep his job, he had to go away to a 30-day treatment facility, Mirmont. I remember those trips because Mirmont was beautiful and serene, and housed on acres of gorgeous land, and for the first time in his life and our marriage, he was coming clean about his secret drug addiction. We learned that both Mrs. Bosman and I were enablers (assisted him in his addiction by supplying him with money and/or making excuses for him). We each attended workshops and support-group meetings (Narcotics Anonymous and Alcoholics Anonymous) to help Mario overcome his addiction. We learned that he had to change the people he hung around with (Kelly included), to the places he frequented (drug houses, bars, friends houses, or trigger spots which encouraged him to indulge in substance abuse), and the things (liquor). We also learned that we had to begin giving him tough love.

I was inspired and extremely hopeful that our marriage could survive this drug and girl problem, and it did for a while. But I had to become his jailer and sit on him to keep him from sneaking out and using drugs or contacting Kelly. Unfortunately, I couldn't do it. I already had one baby to take care of.

Even after that first rehab stay, Mario was still abusing drugs and continuing to sneak around and see Kelly. I believe he wasn't ready to make changes because he hadn't hit his bottom yet, and only went away to save his job. For example, I remember when Mario's brother Artavious married Cathy and we returned home, Mario still clad in his tuxedo from being a groomsman rushed in the house and attempted to sneak out undetected, but I had a surprise for him. Since he never was a true confessor of his feelings for Kelly, I decided to follow him and see for myself. Just like an episode of "Cheaters," and as I suspected, Kelly picked him up, and when she realized I was on to them, she drove to some secluded place and went into the trunk of her car and pulled out an object I couldn't make out and went ballistic! She smashed my rearview window with a tire iron. I thought, "This is sick!" This girl is crazy, but worse yet, I'm just as crazy as she is because here I am following her and now I'm scared silly because I don't even know what she might do or whether Mario has my back because she didn't make him sneak out to be with her. She was all hyped-up as Mario attempted to calm her down. She was yelling expletives as she told me "you had no business following us!" I was beginning to feel like I was the other woman. I hurried back to the safety of my home, not knowing what to do next. I reported the incident to my insurance carrier, telling the representative that I knew exactly who had broken my window, but when it was all said and done, all they were concerned about was their $500 deductible the insured was responsible for. Needless to say, my guilty husband paid the deductible!

(1990) DIVORCE, WELL, IT'S ABOUT TIME

Divorce was inevitable for us because we were leading two separate lives. Our trust had been "irretrievably broken," and our marriage had been a failure from the start. I stayed with Mario throughout two 30-day rehabilitation treatments over the period of several years, hoping that he would finally begin to change his ways, and through his infidelities which could have ended fatally with either one of us contracting Aids or some other infectious disease.

I attempted to seek marriage counseling, but I was the only one participating in the counseling sessions. The therapist, someone from ACORN, provided by our job, helped me realize that I had been afraid of "a failed marriage," when my marriage was already a failure. Truth sets us free. Jesus said to the people who believed in him, *"You are truly my disciples if you keep obeying my teachings. And you will know the truth, and the truth will set you free" (John 8:31–32 NLT).*

I started disvaluing myself by having meaningless affairs with men just to be vindictive towards Mario. "But, the man who commits adultery is an utter fool, for he destroys his own soul. Wounds and constant disgrace are his lot. His shame will never be erased. For the woman's husband will be furious in his jealousy, and he will have no mercy in his day of vengeance. There is no compensation or bribe that will satisfy him" (Proverbs 6:32–35 NLT).

The climax came when I made plans to go out, and on one of those rare occasions when he was home, he wanted me to stay home as well. When I refused, we argued and he attempted to stop me by head-butting me and cracking my tooth and breaking my nose with his head. I was so devastated and embarrassed that I called the police and had him arrested, and I pressed charges, as well as got a restraining order to ensure that he stayed as far away from me as possible. I first sought advice from my employer's legal counsel but learned that their retaining fees were exorbitant, and I couldn't afford to have them represent me, especially since Mario was opposed to a divorce. But I couldn't let that deter me. I was determined to find a lawyer! I consequently located a lawyer in Center City, Philadelphia, who specialized in no-fault divorces and who was not motivated solely by monies, but the needs of his clients charging as little as $250 as long as both parties agreed to the termination of the marriage.

Initially, I filed for divorce a year after his second Rehabilitation, but he refused to comply and sign the divorce papers, choosing to facetiously sign Sammy Davis, Jr. My lawyer who was extremely patient and experienced in these types of outcomes suggested I be patient because through experience he knew that sooner or later Mario would sign, and sure enough, he did. Motivated by monies, he demanded I sell our house. Therefore, I hired a real estate broker, who happened to be my manager at work, the late Everett Smith, to sell our house, but we learned there were liens on the property because of automobile accidents incurred by Mario, and it couldn't be sold until the liens were satisfied. At that point, I proposed buying him out instead for $5,000 in August 1990. Although I didn't have cash monies to buy him out, I opted to get a cash advance from one of my many credit cards. He readily accepted, strung out as he was.

Our son, Mario Brit, who was five years old at the time, had begun parochial school located adjacent to our house. He attended St. Athanasius Immaculate Conception because I wanted him to have a strong moral and religious foundation which I knew I lacked. I was determined to expose him to a more spirit-filled life! As a youngster I attended church with my maternal grandmother frequently, but I didn't get a good enough foundation to nurture him spiritually. At that time, I did not even own a Bible, nor did I know where to begin my instruction, except to teach him what I knew, which wasn't enough.

After my divorce I took stock of my circumstances and admitted to myself I needed to make some major changes, beginning with my fear of change, fear of living alone and the fear of living my life without a partner! I needed to just step out on faith, whatever that was. I didn't like how I looked, my self esteem was in the toilet, and I had a strong concern that no one would want me because I had a child in tow, and money was at a premium! To support my budding belief in myself, I began frequenting neighboring bookstores and grew attracted to the "self-help" section reading all types of positive books, including several by Iyanla Vanzant including, *There's Value in the Valley and, Tapping the Power Within, The Power of Positive Thinking* by Dr. Norman Vincent Peale, *Manifest the Power Within* by Dr. Wayne Dwyer, etc. Luckily, I had the Lord on my side because soon after Mario moved out, my mom needed a place to live.

CHAPTER VIII

AM I MY MOTHER'S KEEPER?

Appearance wise, thinking back, it had to have been the Lord because truthfully speaking being as self-centered as I was, I didn't want to allow mom to live with me because in my twenties I had an image to uphold. I wanted people to know I had my own place, not to believe I was still living at home with mom. However, after the death of my maternal grandmother, Lucille Fitzgerald Stone Pace, on January 12, 1989, my mother who resided just a few doors away, came knocking.

"Bridget, I need a place to stay. Can we (she and her twins, Geneis and Geneva) stay with you until I get a place?"

Shamefully I hesitated and said something to the effect of, "I'll have to think about it!"

Lord, what was I valuing? Am I my mother's keeper? Had it not been for this woman who birthed and cared for me, no telling what would have become of me? Fortunately, I made the correct decision and opened my home up to my mother and twin siblings, and vowed to myself to look out for them the best I knew how. In actuality, they gave me a purpose, and a very strong will to make a difference in all of our lives.

Mom was unemployed, lacking basic saleable skills with no strong desire to work, collecting public assistance for her youngest children, Geneis and Geneva. She applied for public housing in Philadelphia because she had grown accustomed to that type of lifestyle in North Hills, Montgomery County. Fortunately, there was a long waiting list for people seeking public housing in Philadelphia. There were times when I wished for their project (PHA home) to materialize, but for some unknown reason, as fate would have it, years passed and I believe it was God's will that they stayed with me for years, and you know what? It was the best thing because we supported each other as a unit!

As I attended school during the evenings, Mario Brit, needed caring for, and luckily, my mom was there. She also provided assistance with the household chores, not my forte. We actually complemented one another well because what she lacked, I provided, and what I lacked she was there, and we made a dynamic team. She stayed at home and cared for the children and the domestic work, while I went to work to absorb as much education as I could obtain in the eight plus hours I was there, as well as pursuing my dream of a college education through evening studies at LaSalle University

DARKNESS

FEAR   PAIN

CONFUSION

SADNESS

LOST

SECRETS

QUIET

ANGER

HIDING

BROADWAY HERE
I COME

CHAPTER IX

"ALL THE WORLD'S A STAGE" DESIRE TO BE A CORPORATE STAR—REINVENT MYSELF!

On December 17, 1979 I was hired to work in a major gas utility in Philadelphia, Pennsylvania, as a Junior Clerk with Stenography skills, fresh out of business school at eighteen years of age, and I was elated! Lisa and I were about to graduate from the Philadelphia School of Office Training (PSOT) after completing a curriculum for Legal Secretarial Science. Lisa, as expected, obtained a position in our chosen career field as a legal secretary in Radnor, Pennsylvania, and she was showcased by PSOT, because after all, that's what the school trained us to do, and she became a poster child for them! Inwardly, I was a little envious because, as usual, she did everything perfectly because she was so talented! My older sister could dance, draw, sing, and she was so beautiful, too, but I was very proud of her, and happy to say she was my sister!

Although I didn't land a position in my career field, I was also very satisfied with my accomplishment and looking forward to making my mark solo, out of Lisa's shadow, because, after all, we had spent our entire school lives together. In the legal profession there were too many formalities for me, and somehow not having to remember legal jargon was a bit of a relief.

The first few weeks were both exhilarating and sobering because I finally accomplished my mission of getting hired, business school paid off, but I experienced my very first memorable family death, my Aunt Barbara Stone, my mother's middle sister, and her funeral was the first funeral I can remember as an adult that had any real significance. Barb as we affectionately called her was middle aged and in her fifties when she passed from emphysema. She was a beautiful buxom brown woman with very fine, naturally straight long hair, who also shared my mom's mental illness diagnosis throughout her lifetime.

The funeral was extremely sad, especially for Barb's only daughter, Ernestine (Tine), and only son, Tony Stone. Growing up Tine was my role model. I wanted to be just like her. Of course, I would never be as pretty as she, but yet I idolized her. Cousin Tine always shared. She allowed us to wear her clothing, and instructed us on the facts of life (birds and bees), and anything that a parent would provide, her only request was this, "Lisa and Bridget, dust your feet off because I don't want any crumbs in my bed."

INTROVERT

Fortunately, my focus was on starting work, getting promoted, and getting married! But, there was one very serious problem I needed to address. I was extremely shy and introverted, and spoke very rapidly, making it extremely hard for me to be understood. My mother assumed I would grow out of my disposition. Unfortunately, this would not have been so because I shared the same handicap as her, and at sixty-three years of age as the world has changed, she is still introverted and extremely limited in her world!

Getting back to work, my former manager suggested I slow down because I spoke much too rapidly, "and sounded like a chicken," and he said that when I answered his telephone as his secretary his colleagues/callers were complaining that they couldn't understand my dialect.

Obviously I felt insulted, and his comments affected my esteem, and I was extremely embarrassed and blind sighted because I hadn't been critiqued about the way I spoke before. I had never been properly instructed on my speech, my sister Lisa had the speech impediment when we were younger. She used to stutter really badly until she went to speech classes. I wished I could instantly change the way I sounded so that I could sound professional. Business school didn't even offer instruction in dialect. You would have thought that in business school when we were training to become secretaries taking Typing, Shorthand, Accounting, etc., that we would have been instructed in speaking properly. I took his comments to heart, and wished I could immediately attend finishing school, where I could get proper instruction on speaking professionally, etiquette, etc. In his book entitled *Laws of the Spirit*, writer Dan Millan writes that I was out of balance and that the fastest way for me to find my center was to overcorrect—to deliberately practice the opposite of what I was used to doing. For example, if you speak too rapidly or too quietly for people to understand you, then you need to deliberately talk in a way that feels "too slow" and fortunately, my dear Mrs. Bosman (mother-in-law) was interested in helping me to succeed, and began calling me often, suggesting that I begin slowing down and speaking more clearly.

"Bridge," she would say, "you sound much more professional today, and you are going to be somebody. Take your time. Go ahead, girl. I'm going to see you in the *Jet* magazine." She really knew how to boost my self-confidence! Mrs. Bosman had a habit of calling me and asking, "What do you know good?" To which I initially replied, "Nothing." She gently shared a particular scripture, "I can do all things through Christ which strengthens me." And, every time she called thereafter she would chime "what do you know good, Bridge?" And I would recite the magic scripture!

I decided to get on a mission to improve myself. I read everything from *Success Runs in our Race* to *Coach Yourself to Success*, *The Power of Positive Thinking*, *How to Get What You Want and Want What You Have*, and anything in between.

BOOKS CHANGED MY LIFE

I realized I had adopted my parents' beliefs by accident in an Effective Communications, Psychology class in college, and when I went to work, I was very quiet and introverted, like my mother. Too afraid to join in and interact with fellow co-workers, white or black. Fortunately, I discovered a jewel when I went to the Self-Help section of the bookstore and miraculously located a book that would change my life forever entitled, *How to Overcome Shyness* by Jonathan Cheek, which detailed steps I could take to improve my self-esteem, helping me to be able to join in on conversations, and become less consumed by feelings of inadequacies. That book was a Godsend!

I felt like I had my very own tutor. He offers many helpful tips to use in overcoming my inability to speak in various situations. I was able to readily apply his suggestions. Mr. Cheeks describes many techniques for entering into conversations and I practiced his technique called "de-centering" where he suggests that instead of the shy person focusing in on what he/she doesn't have to say (negative thinking), instead change the focus to just listening to what the other person is saying and not being so self-absorbed in what you don't have to say (positive thinking), and I found that it worked wonders for my communication skills.

I began to blossom, and I knew my secret. Books! They changed my life because I saw that I could change anything I desired to.

I was on a mission, a mission to succeed, and next I stumbled onto a packet entitled "Ready, Set, Glow," which basically said that business was a game and broke it down into three categories, Performance-10%, Image-30%, and Exposure-60%, and the theory was that if one could perform well, had a business appearance, was perceived as a team player, had 60% exposure, she/he would be successful.

Performance which only amounted to 10% of the equation outlined the basic theory. The study suggested that "if you didn't know your job, no one would take you seriously." Secretaries definitely needed to know their jobs inside and out, and fortunately high school and business school gave me a strong foundation developing my typing and shorthand abilities.

HIGH SCHOOL AND BUSINESS SCHOOL

By the time I arrived at my place of employment, I had perfected my craft with the repetitious typing tasks administered at Martin Luther King High School (MLK) and Philadelphia School of Office Training (PSOT), "practice, practice, practice, was the instruction of every typing teacher I knew." After all as the cliché goes, "Repetition is the mother of skill."

As a secretary, the dictionary was my right hand, and to become familiar with the typewriter's keyboard, we spent our entire four years of high school in the business curricular and practiced increasing our typing speed by taking timed typing exams which had to contain a minimum of errors.

We were required to master the typewriter's keyboard by looking away from the keys and directly at the material we were typing, and if caught peering at the assigned lesson, the entire class would hear the startling, "Miss Jesse (my maiden name), keep your eyes on your paper, not on your fingertips because it will only slow you down." That was always so embarrassing, especially for an introverted teenager. Unfortunately, I still had a difficult time listening and continued to sneak and peep, and to my detriment because I typed too cautiously and slowly to be at the head of the class, but my sister, Lisa, was a force to be reckoned with, she blazed on the keyboard, even though she would have a trillion mistakes, which would end up reducing her speed. I recall, in order to graduate the program, our typing speed had to be at least fifty-five words per minute with a minimum of errors.

At work I passed the required timed typing tests, which at the time was only forty-five words per minute (wpm) and shorthand at eighty wpm with minimal errors. Hallelujah, I got my foot in the door and hopefully I would never really be required to use my shorthand skills. Luckily, I didn't have to take dictation often, but occasionally some boss would dictate a letter and I would go into a panic! I would panic because I didn't keep up with my speed by practicing all the time, and because I couldn't transcribe accurately what I wrote.

In school we were taught Gregg Shorthand while some girls were taught Pittman Shorthand and were required to only use the exact strokes we learned, not different versions of our own shorthand, but once I was in the real world, and nervous about my inadequacies, I used whatever I could get down on paper! I was sure that many of the bosses knew what they dictated wasn't what I transcribed, and I encountered a few wise-guy managers that made my early years challenging, to say the least.

A favorite story I like to retell is that one of my boss's dictated letters to me, not from his head, while he was thinking aloud, but from a sheet of paper he had written, just to keep me on edge and anxious, as he departed for his two hour lunch with another business colleague. At first I was on edge, but in time I caught on to his little game, and I developed a strategy for overcoming my shorthand dilemma. I discovered where he would leave the paper he read from, and kindly copied it verbatim, and when he would read it, he would be amazed that not only was I speaking more clearly and slowing my speech down, but I took excellent dictation! The joke was now reversed, and on him.

Another example I recall was when I was the secretary to the Affirmative Action manager and my company had formed a new Affirmative Action committee, the head of the Human Resources Department (HR) decided that because I was a "competent secretary with stenography skills," I should take the minutes of the meetings and not be permitted to use a tape recorder like my boss suggested. Needless to say, I was horrified, and hoped I didn't lose my position once I botched up what people said since I was more interested in hearing what people were saying than recording what they were saying. Shorthand was just a way of making money and definitely not my passion. Just like everything in life, I overcame by staying the course and keeping my composure under pressure, and luckily my understanding manager suggested I paraphrase (type up what I thought was said) and send it to the individuals to approve before I compiled the actual minutes for distribution. What a lifesaver he was!

BUILT MY IMAGE

Next, I tackled my image because according to the study it amounted to 30% of the formula and I wanted to be seen as a serious game player. This was easy because I love to shop and, therefore, I began by upgrading my wardrobe, buying clothing on credit and getting further and further in debt. Because I was so miserable at home, this was easy because I rationalized my spending was for a good cause and I had to "fake it before I made it." I charged most everything and loved the attention I got when I wore my new outfits to work. It was ludicrous, I even allowed myself a clothing budget which included anything that was full-priced (not on sale) and that I could pile on my Macy's or Strawbridge's credit card accounts. My account limits were $5,000 and $2000 respectively at 18–21% interest for twenty years. My sister, Lisa, nicknamed me Ms. Macy's and I was content to just charge it because I rationalized it was for a good cause—my career, and besides my home life was in turmoil and it helped relieve stress and depression. I was definitely a shopper, and unfortunately, this was the beginning of my abusing credit cards and carrying much too much debt. In hindsight I could have had thousands of dollars in my bank account had I known better.

I began wearing make-up and became obsessed with changing my hairstyle to develop a more polished look and I always tried to stay clear of bringing my problems to work. Christians should care more about their spiritual welfare than their physical appearance. *"And I want women to be modest in their appearance. They should wear decent and appropriate clothing and not draw attention to themselves by the way they fix their hair or by wearing gold or pearls or expensive clothes. For women who claim to be devoted to God should make themselves attractive by the good things they do"* *(1 Timothy 2:9–10).* Unfortunately, I had no knowledge of this scripture at the time.

Authenticity – genuine, sincere and frank; honest and forthright

In addition to working on my introversion tendencies, I had to work on my authenticity. I had the tendency of attempting to be honest and open with people too quickly, but I knew that if employers/coworkers knew all the details of my life, they would judge me before getting the chance to know me. I felt my childhood was different than others, especially because both parents lost their minds. I felt that if anyone ever found out my secrets they would assume I was mentally ill as well. Unfortunately, I learned quickly that I couldn't level completely with everyone about everything because I didn't want to be judged by where I came from, like the fact that I grew up in the projects. The fact that I couldn't be completely open about my life was a paradox to me because I had always valued being completely authentic. I realized that most adults wore masks to give a different perception of who they are in order to succeed in their careers.

I felt people wouldn't understand because I didn't understand myself, and would possibly judge me and think that I was "crazy."

The subject of mental illness was a taboo subject and never discussed in or outside our family. As a teenager I discovered that not only was the full disclosure of mental illness off limits, but that the language of adults was confusing and often a betrayal of who they truly were under the mask they wore. Not only was Santa Claus, the Easter Bunny and the good Tooth Fairy made up characters, so was almost every adult I encountered. I was perplexed by the insincere/phony behavior of society. At twenty-two years of age in a sophomore English class at LaSalle University in Philadelphia, Pennsylvania, the light bulb suddenly went off in my head when we read an excerpt of William Shakespeare's "All the world's a stage, As You Like It, 1600: meaning life is like a play—we merely go through the stages of our life acting it out," and instantly I identified with it.

JAQUES

All the world's a stage,
And all the men and women merely players:
They have their exits and their entrances;
And one man in his time plays many parts,
His acts being seven ages. At first the infant,
Mewling and puking in the nurse's arms.
And then the whining school-boy, with his satchel
And shining morning face, creeping like snail
Unwillingly to school. And then the lover,
Sighing like furnace, with a woeful ballad
Made to his mistress' eyebrow. Then a soldier,
Full of strange oaths and bearded like the pard,
Jealous in honour, sudden and quick in quarrel,
Seeking the bubble reputation
Even in the cannon's mouth. And then the justice,
In fair round belly with good capon lined,
With eyes severe and beard of formal cut,
Full of wise saws and modern instances;
And so he plays his part. The sixth age shifts
Into the lean and slipper'd pantaloon,
With spectacles on nose and pouch on side,
His youthful hose, well saved, a world too wide
For his shrunk shank; and his big manly voice,
Turning again toward childish treble, pipes
And whistles in his sound. Last scene of all,
That ends this strange eventful history,
Is second childishness and mere oblivion,
Sans teeth, sans eyes, sans taste, sans everything.

The truth in that passage resonated so deeply within that for once in my adult life, I knew how to behave. At work when my coworkers were exchanging niceties of their weekends, I couldn't help but feel excluded because my gut feeling told me that many of the people I worked with could care less when they asked the proverbial questions "how was your weekend? How are you? How's the weather? etc." True or otherwise, because of my upbringing, negative feelings and insecurities I had to transform myself into someone who did not internalize so much doubt and lack of belief in others, and realize that "small talk" was a form of conversing and networking, and that I was indeed holding myself back because of my shyness and lack of knowledge. Suddenly, I became "a student on Broadway at work," and I considered my transformation similar to an acting assignment because I had dreams and aspirations, and I knew in order for me to grow and overcome my insecurities I had to change!

In addition, in a poetry segment in another English course administered at LSU we read Paul Laurence Dunbar's, "We Wear the Mask," and I felt I hit pay dirt because at that point I knew I had to behave my way into the position of my dreams! I became an understudy of all the professional secretaries in the company because at that time, I was only a Typist Clerk with shorthand skills, but I had aspirations of becoming an Assistant to a Vice President. I studied their mannerisms, style of dress, their associations, and became a volunteer to create visibility. I had often heard the expression "fake it until you make it" and that's exactly what I knew I had to do. Rather than feeling like I was behaving like a phony person, I chalked my training/impersonations up to acting the part.

Paul Laurence Dunbar's (1872–1906) "We Wear the Mask"

"We wear the mask that grins and lies,

It hides our cheeks and shades our eyes,—

This debt we pay to human guile;

With torn and bleeding hearts we smile,

And mouth with myriad subtleties.

Why should the world be over-wise,

In counting all our tears and sighs?

Nay, let them only see us, while

We wear the mask.

We smile, but, O great Christ, our cries

To thee from tortured souls arise.

We sing, but oh the clay is vile

Beneath our feet, and long the mile;

But let the world dream otherwise,

We wear the mask!

EXPOSURE

By this time I had mastered the art of becoming a terrific employee and had been promoted to working in the Marketing department as Secretary to Vice President. In Marketing I began volunteering to serve on high profile assignments and various committees around the company, mentoring students in the Career Exploration for Youth (CEY) program, volunteering to be a hostess for various affairs, City Hall Galas and trade fairs or community festivals around the city, and I was sure to get coverage for my efforts because I jumped in front of every camera that snapped a photo, as if they were televising me on the evening news! Of course it helped that I knew the photographer snapping most of the pictures involved in covering our company newspaper.

DARKNESS

FEAR   PAIN

CONFUSION

SADNESS

LOST

SECRETS

QUIET

ANGER

HIDING

IT COSTS BIG
TIME TO PRETEND

CHAPTER X

FINANCIAL BONDAGE: HIGH END-VEHICLES

In essence, I had champagne taste, but beer money! Dating back to 1989, I purchased a used Mercedes 190D and instantly I felt I gained the status of my bosses and peers, never mind that my bank account was empty and I resided in a row house that was in desperate need of repairs, instantly I became someone! At work, I could hear people whispering and wondering about my wealth and who I was. They knew I wasn't a drug dealer because I worked as a clerk alongside them. My boss was shocked that I could afford such a vehicle on my salary and he said as much. He even went so far as to peep inside my driver side window to view the mileage on my odometer. It was actually fun for me to pretend that my car was new because my manager was envious of me, of all people, and inside I really felt insignificant!

COMPOUNDED CREDIT DEBT

My credit card debt was spiraling out of control, but I couldn't stop it because I didn't make enough money to support my lifestyle. In retrospect, I used credit cards because I never had enough money to purchase things I desired, and to me my desire has meant more to me than the cost, no matter how outrageous!

I remember the first time I used credit was through a high finance company chosen for me to use by my dad. I was eighteen years old and wanted to purchase my first car, and he shared with me that I needed to establish credit first, and no one would extend credit for a large ticket item, like a car, without a person first having a track record they could observe first. I continued to establish my credit, purchasing a few cars, department store cards, Visa's, Mastercards, etc., and when I married I co-signed for a few joint cards, until we got divorced!

DIVORCE

After I divorced Mario in 1990, I felt it was a good move to hold on to my credit cards, just in case I needed to use them. And it was a good thing I did because I couldn't afford to keep my son in parochial school, and pay my ex the $5,000 he was now demanding that I pay him for his half of our property. When we purchased Limekiln Pike back in 1981, we only paid a meager $26,500 for it, and if I couldn't give him the $5,000, he wanted to sell my home, and for me and our baby, Mario, to start over in an apartment. Fortunately, there was a lien on the property because of a motor vehicle accident he had, and the property couldn't be sold. And, to get Mario off my back, I borrowed the $5,000 off a credit card, and I'm sure I probably owe thousands of dollars just for making that decision, but I have no regrets, because I had no other option, and would do it again in a heartbeat because the house transferred completely to me, and I was able to have the lien removed, and basically start over again without me ex-husband!

In addition, once we were divorced, my income was drastically reduced and I still had to manage. I'm sure you've heard the stories of being denied credit because of a small income. My credit cards helped keep me afloat and not drown! But, there were other times when I didn't need to use them, but I did. I was accustomed to living "high off the hog" as my grandmother used to say. And that desire for instant gratification developed from my father, and I saw what happened to them. We lost our home in a Sheriff Sale, when my dad had his breakdown. I believe it could've been due to too much pressure. I believe my mom's breakdown was a result of her being unable to care for us and pay the bills when my father left!

EXPENSIVE CLOTHING

Flashback to dressing for success in the countless suits I leased/purchased (credit card debt) at the original tag price (not even the sale price) to represent who I thought I had become "a successful businesswoman." In my closet sat tons of clothing I would no longer have need for. My dry cleaner might end up closing her doors or at least feel the loss of my $100 per week dry cleaning bill

DARKNESS
FEAR   PAIN
CONFUSION
SADNESS
LOST
SECRETS

QUIET

ANGER

HIDING

CHAPTER XI

RELATIONSHIP WITH SUAVE CLARK

I dated several men after my divorce from Mario, but one of the more noteworthy was the relationship I had with a professional by the name of Suave Clark, whom I met through a mutual acquaintance. As our relationship progressed I had visions of us sharing a future together, but it couldn't last and this I knew in my gut… He was an old-school player! Suave was ten years my senior, and seemed to enjoy the idea of being an eligible bachelor! Our marital situations were similar. He was currently happily divorced with one son, James, that resided with his ex-wife and he definitely didn't want any more children! That was terrific because I didn't want to have any more children either, unless I was married, so just in case, I continued to use birth control.

The problem with Suave was he seemed a little bit too self-assured and contrived, and it appeared to me as though he got a kick out of trading up women, as if we were trading cards. He traded up to me on New Year's Eve, driving up to my house in a newer model car he had traded up to that very day, his dream Cadillac, when just yesterday he was driving some sort of jalopy announcing that he had ended his relationship with Stephanie because she wasn't meeting his expectations. She didn't appeal to him any longer because she wasn't as sexy as he found me to be. It was okay for me because I loved the attention he was bestowing on me, but I did feel sorry for Stephanie and wanted to help her overcome her lack of sexiness because she seemed to be still in love with him, but he simply cancelled her out for me. His pet name for me was "his young tenderloin." He often shared stories of his past relationships of how they weren't cute enough, or didn't have the style or flavor he found in me. I listened intently, but in my opinion he seemed to go through women at least once every so often.

Intellectually, he was tops, very smart and extremely articulate and he helped me over many rough patches, in college and at work, even though I considered him a bit of a control freak! He supported my desire to volunteer to serve on various committees at school, and we shared the same vision for excelling in the corporate world through exposure and corporate politics. He was a sophisticated gentleman who had a way with words, an extremely eloquent communicator. But I went along with his controlling demeanor for the time being because as he put it, "We all had idiosyncrasies we had to determine whether we could accept about one another." I decided I could adjust to his temperament because I enjoyed the time we spent together and it felt like a retreat just to get away from the hustle and bustle of raising a son alone, and having my mom and twin siblings, Geneis and Geneva, in tow.

I traveled many miles to be with him almost every weekend. He had only recently traded up his style of living from living in a row house in the Northeast section of Philly and purchased his dream rancher in Williamstown, New Jersey.

However, my son, Mario, who was ten years old at the time didn't really bond with him. His dad, Mario Corvette, and I had been divorced for nearly five years, but it seemed he was hoping that his dad and I would reconcile, even though I knew this would never be so! I had my heart set on settling down and marrying someone so that I could spend more time at home with him. There were times when I preferred to stay home with my child, and that's what I did, but it caused friction in our relationship. Spending so much time away from my offspring in order to find a suitable mate was truly a factor that kept me in the relationship with his dad for as long as I was. Fortunately, Suave was a very enterprising man and always seemed to be busy doing one thing or another. He did taxes on the side, and repaired houses when the tax business slowed down.

Unfortunately, as a single mother, I had to date and get to know my partner if I were to find my prince (Mr. Right). At first I was extremely cautious and didn't introduce every one of my male friends to Mario because I wasn't sure where the relationships were going, and I certainly didn't entertain at home. Fortunately for me, my mother, Geneis and Geneva lived with us and kept Mario occupied I rationalized.

My relationship with Suave began to fizzle after I graduated from college over something as silly as a graduation party I proposed to throw for myself. He objected to the idea of me hosting a gala on the *Spirit of Philadelphia* for thirty-five of my closest family and friends because he considered it too much of an expenditure. Unfortunately, I hosted a beautiful affair and he refused to attend, but instead he hosted a small informal barbeque at his home in Williamstown, and after the boat ride on the *Spirit of Philadelphia* I, along with a few of my friends, made an appearance at his barbeque. Unfortunately, our relationship went downhill after that!

As fate would have it, I ended up pregnant, and neither he nor I desired a baby at that time, and we chose to abort our child. Unfortunately, I had that one final abortion! That abortion led me to my physician, who chastised me saying that "Children are a gift from God." "Children are a gift from the Lord; they are a reward from him" (Psalm 127:3).

He said, "Bridget, do you not know that your body is made in the image of God? Don't you know that your body is your temple? Why would you terminate your child? If there's a next time, there will be no terminating the pregnancy. My church will raise the child."

At this point, the relationship between Suave and I was too strained and sex became non-existent because I could no longer take birth control and I dared not get pregnant.

CHAPTER XII

ACCEPTANCE OF JESUS CHRIST AS
MY LORD AND SAVIOR

Quite sometime later on Easter Sunday 1995, after the breakup of my relationship with Suave Clark, I was hurting deeply and suffering emotionally with no place left to turn. I confided in my big sister how I was feeling, so she invited me to come along with her to church. Lisa had been enjoying her new "saved" life in a non-denominational church, Calvary Assembly of God, where the church van picked her and her son, Terrance, up for worship, and she sang to her hearts content on the Adult Choir. Before service even began, she ushered me in to speak with Pastor Williams. I shared with him my uncertainty about being "saved from the pits of hell" and about my relationship with Christ. I wasn't sure whether I needed to make a public confession regarding my belief in our Lord and Savior before the church. Pastor Williams prayed a special prayer over me and encouraged me to invite the Lord into my heart, believing that He died for my sins, which I did, and took my seat for a life changing service. The pastor gave a most heartfelt sermon, after which, during altar call with all eyes shut, he invited believers who desired to be saved to walk in faith to the front of the church. As if in a trance, I found myself gliding down the aisle, making my public confession before the entire congregation in a waterfall of tears, my belief in the Lord and was instantly, saved and found a peace that passes all understanding and a heavy burden being lifted!

CHAPTER XIII

ANOTHER CHANCE AT LOVE — MY PRINCE CHARMING

(1997)

I met David at a nightclub of all places, and instantly I felt a connection, as if fate had her hand in creating our union. We were at a now defunct club and we all know how difficult it is to marry someone you meet at a nightclub! I struck up a conversation with him because Tine recognized him from Crestmont, a small suburban town in Willow Grove, Pennsylvania. He knew Tine, but had never laid eyes on me, and we ended up talking all evening long regarding the multitude of my relatives he knew, all residing in Crestmont. The meeting was so magical that he ended up taking us to Breakfast at IHOP. I couldn't believe my luck because most of the guys I had been meeting were cheap, and David was looking very handsome and debonair in his sky blue suit. We walked to his black Diamante, which he had parked on the rooftop of the night club, and I took one look at him and his car, and claimed him and the front seat to Tine and a friend Selma Cooper, whether they were interested or not, I knew this man would be mine. He was a little slow to the altar, two years, and because my biological clock was ticking, I was thirty-six years old, and I had to coach him along.

I dated David for a few years, but our relationship didn't seem to be going in the direction I had hoped it would be going in, so we broke up. I began dating an older gentleman who seemed to offer me the support, security, and guidance I longed for. In addition to enjoying his company, he had loads of wisdom and life experiences to offer, more knowledge than even my father seemed to have, and I'm sure that played a part in our relationship. However, not long after David and I broke up, we had a heart-to-heart discussion about where our relationship was headed, and what we both desired to have in our lives. A few days later, he called me and said that he would like to see me and had an offer that I couldn't refuse, and if I did decide to refuse it, he would vacate my life for good. We got together and he presented me with a beautiful one carat oval-shaped diamond ring and asked me to marry him! I was speechless! I accepted David's marriage proposal because I love him and I knew we could build a life together.

(1997) MARRYING THE MAN OF MY CHOICE, DAVID VAN BUREN TURNER

"For better for worse, for richer for poorer, in sickness and in health" is the part of the wedding vow that is usually said during one of the happiest day's of one's life but is sometimes taken for granted. Three years after I wed my husband, David, the shock he must have felt when suddenly I couldn't walk and was diagnosed with mixed connective tissue diseases! It was a traumatic situation to say the least and he could have walked away from our marriage. After all, we were still ironing out the creases in our relationship and our marriage to me was dim in comparison to the excitement of our romantic wedding day!

However, very early on when I couldn't walk and physicians couldn't tell me for sure whether I would walk again, learned my diagnosis, he held me in his arms, looked me in my eyes, and assured me that I didn't have to worry about him leaving me, and that he just wanted me to concentrate on getting well! I gained a tremendous amount of faith in David and hope for our renewed marriage commitment during this "winter" season of my life, and I could pinch myself because he really did love me and he genuinely cared. Early on I couldn't get a clear reading on his feelings. At times in our marriage, I simply wasn't sure because he was not as open nor vocal as I needed him to be, plus I would sometimes get flashbacks of my past failed marriage and bring my insecurities to my new life with David. I loved the fact that he was there for me physically and emotionally and was able to keep up on my health issues by conversing with the physicians and hospital staff. I believe David and I were meant to be together.

My true prince charming has arrived. Not the prince you read about in the fairytales, but a God fearing man with great character, wisdom and principles and honors the vows he took to me.

We married almost ten years ago and we have been going through major life events ever since. The day we married, my son Mario, who was thirteen at the time, and I left the Marriott early to shop for school clothing for the upcoming school year at the Rose Uniform Shop in Willow Grove. As we were waiting to purchase his uniforms I began to feel somewhat dizzy, and the next thing I knew, boom! I fell to the floor and fainted! Shocked, I opened my eyes a few seconds later after someone had thoughtfully placed a peppermint in my mouth. .I looked at Mario and asked, "What happened." As he explained what happened, I knew instantly that I was pregnant because each time I found myself carrying a child, one of the very first symptoms was I'd faint. I told the concerned lookers on at the uniform shop that "today's my wedding and it's extremely hot outside, and I'm excited. I'm okay; we're staying at the Courtyard at the Marriott up Route 611, right up the street. I'm fine," and we left to get dressed and join our bridal party back at the hotel. Excitedly, we returned to the Marriott and shared the news with my big sister Lisa who in turn shared the news with everyone. Lisa was so overjoyed for me, so caring and concerned, and couldn't wait to be an aunt one more time.

We had our marriage ceremony at the hometown church, the First Baptist of Crestmont, and our color scheme were various shades of the royal color of purple because purple is David's favorite color. Lisa Jesse (sister) and Tine Stone (cousin) were my maids of honor, and Marilyn (Putt) Lawton Jenkins, Doris Graham, and Jackie Moody Houser, all my very best friends, and two of David's five sister's, Donna and Dawn Vaughn, were my bridesmaids. David's best buddies flew in from all over to be there for him. His best friend Guy Baron flew in from Colorado, Cal and Thurman came from Florida, Donald Vaughn (Yogi), David's brother, came from Maryland, Keith Holland (cousin), New Jersey and Gino,

Philadelphia. I marched in with my dad, who was showing signs of stress as he was stepping on my train as we waltzed (walked) to the wedding march being played on saxophone by my very own talented son, Mario. I was concentrating on my father just at least giving me away and not ruining my day, and thankfully he didn't! The sacred ceremony was too beautiful not to cry! I believe us girls couldn't help but smear our mascara. I was so happy because this time both my parents were there.

As father-of-the-bride, my dad gave me away, but I was on pins-and-needles because I knew our secret, he had been exhibiting signs of another breakdown! He had not been taking his medication for his condition and it was starting to show. My dad's mental history went back his entire lifetime so we were prepared, however, I had been hoping/praying that he was well enough to give me away, and then the fallout from his lack of medication could occur, and fortunately, my wish came true! To the majority of our guests, he appeared like the normal father-of-the-bride, a little nervous, but to his family, we knew about the dark side, and I feared the worse, but it was over and I had my new husband, and I was prepared to begin my new life!

At the reception Lisa was so full of life, joy and happiness! She wasn't a professional singer by any stretch of the imagination, more like an American Idol contestant, and ever since we were younger we enjoyed belting out tunes. As kids we both sang in the local talent competitions, and at our grandmother, Morn's church, United Church of the First Born in Germantown. In high school, Lisa even had the courage to sing Phoebe Snow's song, "No Regrets" in a Gong Show competition, and she wasn't gonged. That's why it came as no surprise that she would even want to sing in front of 200 guests with no singing lessons. But my big sister, Lisa, sang Phyllis Hyman's "The Answer Boy is You" and she sang from her heart and we felt happy and considered it a genuine gift, even though the actual singing was a little off key, she sang for me and my new husband, David!

CHAPTER XIV

MY SISTER LISA'S DEATH

(1998)

Six months later when I was pregnant with my second child, on February 10, 1998, I received a telephone call at work. Ring Ring Ring. "Hello, is this Bridget, Bridget Turner?"
"Yes, this is she."
"This is Diane from Queen Lane Housing, and I got your number from your sister's rolodex. I work with your sister, Lisa, and I was asked to give you a call because we were eating lunch and all of a sudden she started choking on something she ate, some Chinese food we had for lunch, and well, some food got stuck in her throat and she started choking and was taken to the hospital."
"Is she okay?"
"Oh, yes, they just took her there as a precaution."
"Who took her?"
"We called 911, and an ambulance took her."
"Would you be able to accompany her at the hospital?"

"Sure, I'll be right there, what hospital?"

I jokingly notified my manager that I had been summoned to the hospital because I had received a call from Lisa's coworker and apparently she was in a hurry to eat and ate hastily and the food went down the wrong pipe. I told him I would be back as quickly as I could because the hospital was not that far away, about fifteen minutes on Erie Avenue.

I had been expecting to see my sister later, either at my house or at her home anyway because I wanted to give her only son, my nephew, Terrance, a present for his sixteenth birthday, which just so happened to be that day, February 10, 1998.

On the drive to the hospital I was anticipating seeing my older sister, imagining that she would be laughing and talking up a storm because she was so bubbly and effervescent, and saying something like, "Bridget, girl, guess what happened to me..." The idea that she was in the hospital at all was highly unusual for Lisa because she always seemed so healthy and vibrant. Even though over the years after she had Terrance she had steadily gained weight, but it never seemed to be a problem. I knew my sister would be so glad to see me, and that she would light up when she saw me arrive, so I hurried to the emergency room where she would be waiting to be released and accompanied home by me because she loved me in that wonderful way only an older sister felt about her younger siblings.

I arrive at the hospital and am immediately greeted by one of Lisa's coworkers who rode alongside her to the hospital and we're ushered in to a family waiting room, lined with comfy padded chairs and a television set, and asked to have a seat. At once I'm alarmed and yet curious wondering why I'm asked to take a seat. Is it because I'm seven months pregnant and showing? I've been asked to take a seat I think! No, something's not right. "Where's my sister, where's Lisa?"

"The doctor will be right in to talk to you."

My heart starts pounding, thump, thump, thump.

Her coworker is friendly and comforting and sharing that "Lisa was so happy today. She was really excited and planning a nice birthday celebration for Terrance, and she was also planning a baby shower for you..."

"Are you a relative of Lisa Jesse?"

"Yes."

"I'm sorry to tell you, your sister didn't make it!"

"What?"

"She died."

Oh no, I begin to silently weep. "Did she die from choking off her food? I thought I was told that she was alright, and I was called as a matter of protocol."

"I am extremely sorry for your loss, is there anyone else that needs to be notified?"

"Yes, her only son, Terrance!"

"If you need to contact anyone, please feel free to use the telephone."

In shock and total disbelief I reply, "Oh no, it's his sixteenth birthday, and I'm sure he's waiting for her to come home and celebrate, and now he's going to hear this."

I immediately spring in to action, telephoning everyone in my phonebook who I knew would want to know, and could help me through this horrible ordeal. I phoned my husband, my cousin Tine, best friends Putt and Doris, Jackie, Terrance's dad, Lewis, and my mom, Geneva Jesse. Since Terrance was at home alone, and was trained to not open the door or answer from anyone other than Lisa. I wasn't able to readily call my dad because he was suffering his own personal demons and was hospitalized.

 Coincidentally, both my dad and my younger sister Geneva were both in Friend's Mental Hospital when Lisa passed away, suffering breakdowns. My dad had such a long history of these breakdowns, whereas Geneva had been newly diagnosed.

 It was mind-boggling to me because an autopsy performed on Lisa ruled that her cause of death was cardiovascular disease and morbid obesity. Lisa died at only thirty-seven years of age, just one year older than me, and weighed 315 lbs, information that she had never shared with me while living. We had discussed walking and buying sneakers, but never followed through on it. Months before she passed she shared that she was satisfied with her size, and that "the only reason she would lose weight was for her health," which makes me wonder whether her physician forewarned her of the danger of her being overweight. If we could go back, I would caution Lisa to change her diet and exercise.

CHAPTER XV

DAVID TURNER III'S BIRTH (1998)

Two months later, on April 18, 1998, our precious baby boy, David Van Buren Turner III, was born weighing seven lbs. six ounces. His birth was melancholy for me because I was happy he was born, but sad that Lisa, who I had spent my entire life with, was gone and not there to share her tales and pure laughter with me. I nursed David, something I hadn't been successful at during my previous childbirth with Mario thirteen years prior, but he was a hungry little "boobie" and sucked me dry for over thirteen months as I returned to work drained all the time. Because I wanted to be the absolute best mother I could be and give my child a really good start, I believe I put myself at risk for what was about to come.

DARKNESS

FEAR   PAIN

CONFUSION

SADNESS

LOST

SECRETS

QUIET

ANGER

HIDING

CHAPTER XVI

YES, I AM MY MOTHER'S KEEPER

After my acceptance of Jesus Christ as my Lord and Savior I became even more determined to live my life the correct way. I had long before accepted my responsibility of looking after my mom. Fortunately, I have been very involved in my mother's life and she has not had a breakdown in well over twenty-five plus years, thank God! She began worshipping at Mt. Airy Church of God and to relieve my mom, Geneva, of the "voices," hallucinations and delusions she was having, she was prescribed various anti psychotic medications in the early years of her diagnosis, including haloperidol (Haldol) and fluphenazine (Prolixin), and she had many relapses, and finally successfully prescribed perphenazine (Trilafon), and Cogentin to counteract the side effects, i.e. tremors, restlessness, muscle spasms.

For years she/we applied for public housing, even with the assistance of my sister Lisa, working as a secretary at the Philadelphia Housing Department's (PHA) Queen Lane facility, and was always given one excuse or another about being some number on the waiting list, or about missing out on housing opportunities because of her wanting to live in particular Philadelphia locations, etc., until miraculously, it seemed by divine intervention, I announced I was getting remarried, and then bam—a PHA house is assigned to her!

The move was destined, and for once in her lifetime she had her very own place! Hallelujah! The move was bittersweet because I was extremely excited because I was getting married and could finally start my life off anew with David, my new husband, but then by her moving and me being accustomed to having her around, and the distance was farther than I had hoped for, a thirty to forty-five minute commute to Holmesburg, Pennsylvania, from our home in West Oak Lane, Pennsylvania.

However, during this transition, my sister Lisa and I continued to support her emotionally and financially when she needed it, and assisting her with what ever needed to be done because this was the very first time she was on her own, after all it does take a village to raise children and she still had her twins, who would be completing their high school educations.

After I returned to work after the birth of my second child, I commuted to and fro picking mom up to care for him. The task was arduous, time-consuming and draining physically, but I did it because we needed him to be in the care of family at that critical age. Reflecting back, how much more convenient would it have been had she continued to live with us.

Once I retired on disability, I was able to purchase a second-hand vehicle for her and the reaction I received from my mom was priceless. Her eyes lit up like diamonds, the enthusiasm she exuded came across as if I had given her a million dollars; as opposed to the fifteen hundred dollars it took for her to drive her car. Unfortunately, the upkeep it took for her to maintain the vehicle was too costly and she ended up giving it to David. Hey, for a moment it did take the burden of chauffeuring her to and from and to her appointments and errands off me.

In addition, I have helped keep my mom from relapsing for well over twenty years because she lacked a support system. She would customarily have an episode every few years. By her moving in with me she routinely visits her doctors. There was one incident I can recall where my mom was beginning to act strange, like she was relapsing into having a breakdown again before my eyes. I immediately scheduled an appointment with her psychiatrist, and discovered that the reason she was acting different was because the dosages she was taking had been lowered, and asked him to keep her on the old dosage, he conceded and she improved, thank God.

Income wise, she was receiving public assistance DPA when the twins were growing up, but then we applied for Social Security Disability (SSI) because of her mental illness, and once my father passed, we applied for his pension, and she was awarded her part because she was married to him for seventeen years.

She manages her bills, prescription medicine being her biggest expense because she has no prescription plan, because she never worked any where for too long, her debt consists of a student loan which she acquired after attending a nursing school, even though it should have been free because she was on public assistance. She received a certificate and worked for a while, until she began having difficulties lifting the patients. Because she couldn't handle the responsibilities of the position, she was asked to resign.

When she was living in Liddenfield Homes, Holmesburg, she began having respiratory problems after having been admitted into Frankford Hospital a few times because my younger siblings, twins Geneis and Geneva, along with my nephew Terrance Jesse were no longer residing with her, we made the decision for her to give up her place and move back into our home on Limekiln Pike. It was a terrific decision because it allows me to help my mom plan for her future.

As I recover from my health crisis, my mother Geneva Jesse has been a vital part of my recovery team. She helps me with the daily grind of grueling housework and the myriad other domestic chores involved with caring for a child; after all, she is the doting grandmother of David.

What I have discovered is that I am my mother's keeper, and neither I nor God would want it any other way, and I am very proud of that!

CHAPTER XVII

Death of my Daddy — William Jesse (2000)

My dad died on August 18, 2000. He had been sick for a while now and he was in Abington Hospital hooked up to all types of machines to help him breath and not feel pain. He had many ailments, but he was dying of lung cancer, and it was extremely painful to watch. My dad withered away in size. In the beginning he knew me, but in the end I wasn't so sure. Gone was his beautiful manicured head of hair. I was amazed that he spent so much time during his lifetime to keep his hair looking good, but then in death it retreated like he was fresh from his mother's womb. He called out the names of his brothers as if he was a child again and he saw them over yonder. In the end, his wife, my stepmother, her sister, and I were there.

His second marriage was really good for him because

they had a lot in common; he was a very articulate successful executive, rising to the position of Director, Environmental Services Laundry and Dietary at the Shriner's Hospital for Crippled Children where he retired in 1979. My dad promoted enthusiasm, education and set goals for himself and my stepmother met him halfway. My dad was the head of our family and did everything he could to make a difference in our lives, and he succeeded. He died with dignity in Abington Hospital from lung cancer, and I visited him when I got off work in the evenings until his death.

He is my hero and role model because he never stayed down in life for too long. Life is full of obstacles and takes so many turns and hits you really hard that it's easy to stay down when you're discouraged, people talk about you and you feel ashamed, poke fun at your failures and foibles, when everyone I know has had and will have trouble through their own fault or sometimes someone else's. He had seizures from epilepsy and painful breakdowns, but he never gave up.

When he accepted Christ, I began to see a change in him. Fortunately for us, my stepmother was a praying wife, and helped my dad with his transition to salvation. They worshipped at Calvary Assembly of God together, and planned many of our new family traditions around assembling at church and dining at their home or some fabulous restaurant where he always imparted his wisdom about how we should be conducting our lives, saving money, not incurring too much debt raising our children.

One of the more memorable gifts he and his wife gave me and Lisa was our very first Bibles that he was thoughtful enough to inscribe. As children, Lisa and I attended church most every Sunday with Morn, and we also attended

Antioch Baptist Church in North Hills where we were baptized I believe on Christmas Eve, but I have no recollection of our parents ever attending with us, except on special occasions or Christmas or Easter. Needless to say, it appeared theylacked faith. Because our parents were our first role models, we believed what they taught us. I am sure we believed in our father, William Jesse, and not our father our Lord and Savior, Jesus Christ!

Thank God we grew older and wiser, and when we saw the change in our dad, we were impacted as well. Lisa, who had been going through her own problems and fighting her demons, experienced a change because she and Terrance later joined that very same church, Calvary Assembly of God, and joined the choir where she brought all the soul she could muster to the predominantly Caucasian church. She was later asked to "tone down her soul," but the point I'm making here is that our dad set the stage for our salvation.

I am happy that in the end my daddy received Christ, as well as obtained his mansion. "In my father's house are many mansions, if it weren't so, I would have told you." He was happily married and he and his wife had an extremely good life together, but I am sorry for the loss. I miss the chats we had and the wisdom he shared.

DARKNESS

FEAR   PAIN

        CONFUSION

SADNESS
                    LOST

SECRETS

                        QUIET

ANGER

            HIDING

CHAPTER XVIII

WHEN ARE WE RELOCATING?

One of the largest hurdles for me and David to overcome was to purchase a home together! I had been living in the same house I originally purchased with my ex-husband, and once we divorced I bought him out, but I felt very stagnate and anxiously desired to move. I longed to be inspired, I truly felt I needed to move in order to grow, and as a couple, I hoped we could establish a foundation together. When I dated David he was living in a beautiful luxury apartment complex in Center City living the way I imagined we would but I felt I lived in a dump! I was so ashamed of where I lived, that I always ached to move.

I dreamed of living in a single home to match what I felt would be an indication of where I was in life, but I was broke, spiritually, mentally, and financially as well! David seemed to be more satisfied with the mortgage and the upkeep being more manageable than keeping up with the Joneses or having a very high mortgage. But, of course, after we married I discovered that he had a five year plan, which turned into a ten-year plan, I hit the ceiling! Life became unbearable until I read something that seemed to describe our family's situation and offered some suggestions on ideas I could incorporate into my very own life.

I came up with a plan to improve the quality of our home! I must have invested well over $30,000. I started with replacing the concrete pavement I detested, and wow what a difference that made in the way I felt about my home. Next, I hired Window Wizards to install windows and steel doors throughout our home, installed fresh carpeting because our Shetland Sheepdog, Lexis, had many accidents on the old rug; purchased a brown leather living room set, replaced the artwork on the walls, upgraded the electrical/lighting fixtures, replaced the ancient oil heater to prevent possible leaky carbon monoxide poisoning, installed a water filter system to prevent drinking possible lead in the water, hired a few handy men to finish the basement allowing a more modern environment for our young son, David, to entertain, and play his video games. We painted, purchased a few personal computers and desks so that we would have our very own personal space to work and be creative at home, changed the bedrooms, and then suddenly... the urge to move, and buy big was gone!

Truly, what I had desired was quality and comfort, not a single home after all. All I really wanted was a home I would be proud of, proud enough to invite friends over, and not feel ashamed of.

Now that I'm retired and our mortgage and taxes are a factor and very low and manageable, I'm able to have the lifestyle that I always desired as well as able to pay my bills. Ever since the house on Limekiln Pike has been refurbished, the quality of living hasn't stopped; it actually extends outside to pride of ownership. We've done some landscaping, thanks to my eldest son, Mario (the one with the green thumb, thanks to his enriching experience at William B. Saul High School). We have tulips and azaleas in the springtime, I am able to walk our dog, Lexis, and I am more in-touch with my community (neighbors), sharing niceties of the day. Now I consider our home our condo!

    I still desire to move, however, when people ask me when I'm moving now, I say, "I'm not in a rush to move because I love my place!"

WALLOWING
IN SELF-PITY

CHAPTER XIX

...HELP, I CAN'T WALK!

LOSS OF HOPE

(2001)

There I lay; incapacitated, stretched out on a sterilized gurney wearing nothing except the standard blue and white polka dotted hospital gown I had been issued expectantly awaiting something miraculous to occur! At only thirty-nine years of age I'm totally deflated, like a hot air balloon with all the life sucked out of it, feeling hopeless and withdrawn, humbled by the predicament I find myself in, with nothing left but the memories of my life. I'm unable to walk (not even to use the bathroom), and I'm even having difficulty utilizing the utensils to feed myself. What happened? Was I going insane like my dad and mom had? Who was I? Did I leave a legacy for my children? Had I accomplished my life's mission or did I even have one? Was I being punished by God? What was the meaning of my life? Why me Lord?

My hospital room seemed surreal and eerily silent, as if I were a part of someone else's nightmare or perhaps returning from their coma because I couldn't readily recall details of my existence. Was it all the medication the physicians were prescribing just to get me through the difficult days and torturous nights, or was it because I wasn't ready to deal with the truth of the situation I found myself in, shocked and not wanting to face my reality! Why couldn't I command my legs, feet and hands to move?

...Daddy, I can't walk! But, then you're gone, you passed away over a year ago in August 2000, and Lisa (my beloved older sister), I know you would be here at my hospital bedside as well, but you passed on February 10, 1998, on Terrance's sixteenth birthday, just six months after David and I married, and two months before David, III was born...I never would have imagined something like this occurring. I was looking forward to my "life beginning at forty," but then I've heard emotional stress can trigger all sorts of reactions...I am lying in the hospital paralyzed in both legs, not able to walk or feed myself. But just yesterday I was so full of life! How could this happen to me? What sort of catastrophe had befallen me, and why was God punishing me? What had I done? And why was it that my temperature was elevated to over 103 degrees, and the slew of physicians coming in and out of my hospital room, who were supposedly trained and educated couldn't even come up with a diagnosis! Up until this point, I believed doctors and hospitals were able to make people well or at least better, but as the days grew long, I was growing weary and confused. The doctor (Gastroenterologist) who admitted me to the hospital originally admitted me because he thought there was blood in my stool, I had a fever, and because my husband had to carry me in to the hospital. Because the physicians didn't know what was wrong with me I began to panic, and I became more and more frightened and thought the worst. Could this be terminal? Did I have cancer, HIV or Aids, or worse? The suspense was driving me insane. I began to recognize then that God was in complete control because there was no one else for me to turn to. I turned inward and became deeply withdrawn and I became more and more depressed. I couldn't believe that a loving God would allow me to become crippled! What had I done, Lord? I felt angry, confused and dejected.

I had often heard the expression "doctors practice medicine," but I never thought I would be in the situation to witness them practicing on me. Because of a few physicians' inexperience and/or lack of knowledge, I was subject to endure quite a bit of experimentation and discomfort. As I whimpered and complained, I learned that they didn't want to prescribe medicine without diagnosing what was actually wrong! Where are you God?

It was near the end of the summer, August 2001, and I had only recently returned to work, to a career I built from the ground up as a Buyer/Purchasing Agent of a major gas utility in Philadelphia, after birthing, David Van Buren Turner, III, a beautiful healthy, seven lb. six ounce baby boy. His birth was much easier than my older son's (Mario) was, besides being thirteen years prior when I was twenty-four years old. I delivered Mario using natural childbirth which was a huge mistake I allowed his dad to talk me into because the pain and delivery were extremely intense, and afterward I couldn't even breast feed him because I developed some type of an infection. Contrarily, at the seasoned age of thirty-seven, David's birth was much simpler because

I had been administered drugs, a.k.a. an epidural anesthetic, which made his delivery feel more like I was watching his birth on a television monitor as opposed to delivering him vaginally. I was able to nurse David, for at least thirteen months, to be certain he received a healthy start in his precious little life, but honestly he must have zapped me completely dry with all the extra sucking he was doing. I was always so physically drained and exhausted even after trying to eat right and taking multiple supplements, but nothing seemed to work. In addition, when I returned home from a long day at the office, I drove my mom, who had been babysitting David, (about an hour commute) home.

Three months later when my maternity leave was over, I returned to work tired all the time, feeling sluggish and rundown and thought the exhaustion may have been related to my age, or perhaps as a result of my nursing him for so long. Work, admittedly, was somewhat stressful these days because I had been going through personality clashes with a particular new Hispanic female director who had been promoted through the ranks, and was flexing her muscles while getting under everyone's skin rearranging everything as she fixed things that weren't even broken! For example, she reassigned me to supervise Office Services, disregarding the myriad of supplies and commodities I was responsible for purchasing. As a result, several months later, I ended up having to reapply for my original position as Purchasing Agent.

Meanwhile, as I look back there were warning signs that something wasn't quite right. All of a sudden I couldn't wear any of my shoes. I recall going shopping and having to purchase an eight and a half instead of my regular seven and a half. I attributed it to childbirth. I incessantly complained to friends and coworkers, "I'm always so tired. I feel completely exhausted and drained; I need to take a break."

I decided to take a break from work and spend some quiet time with my family. Since my husband David and/or my mom Geneva was watching baby David, I was free to relax and enjoy my day. I purchased tickets for Great Adventure for me, my older son Mario, his girlfriend, and my cousin Tine Stone and her daughter Aqueelah, and away we went. We had a wonderful time riding through the safari viewing the animals, even though the chimpanzees were a little frightening as they jumped all over our car, but the park was another story. I decided to do something completely out of the ordinary for me, ride the roller coaster, the scariest ride there of all things, the Batman and Robin, especially one that was advertised as extremely fast. Once we took off, I was terrified! Too late to jump off, the buckle was fastened securely. The train sped so fast that it rattled my brain, and I was visibly shaken. I don't know what I was trying to prove because when I was younger I would have never in a zillion years even attempted to ride a roller coaster! After the Batman roller coaster came to a screeching halt, instantly I developed a migraine headache that I couldn't shake off. I popped Tylenol every four hours. Lord, what was I thinking when I decided to ride a roller coaster? I must've been crazy! "Never again, I exclaimed!"

By that weekend, I was really sick. I felt nauseated and began running a fever. I couldn't explain it, but I felt that my sudden illness had something to do with that Batman roller coaster I had ridden, and I told that to the physicians on duty in the Emergency Room. The physician casually suggested I take Motrin, and sent me home to recuperate. Once I returned home I continued to take the Motrin to relieve discomfort. However, a few days later I returned to work as usual, but then my calves began to stiffen. I recall my supervisor, Ken Williams, saying something to the effect of, "Bridget you're walking like you're an old woman," and I replied, "Yeah, I feel like one."

Well, that conversation took place during the day, and by that evening in late August 2001 I developed a very high temperature, stomach pain, and leg weakness, and found myself attempting to crawl up the stairwell at home. Luckily, my nephew, Angelo Bosman, Jr., was at my house playing video games with Mario, and seeing me struggling he offered to assist me. "Aunt Bridget, would you like some help getting upstairs?"

I cried out, "I can hardly walk." And Angelo carried me up the stairs and deposited me onto my bed. Thinking that I was experiencing some type of stomach virus, my family rallied around me, catering to my every need dispensing Motrin, fixing soup and oatmeal, and assisting me to the bathroom where I attempted to bathe, and ended up perspiring and falling asleep. I became drained and developed diarrhea with an elevated temperature. My husband, David, ended up taking me to Chestnut Hill Hospital's Emergency Room, where just a few years prior I was happily delivering our child, David!

Once I arrived at the emergency room triage unit, it was determined that my temperature was elevated and I was very dehydrated, thus I was given liquids and antibiotics and sent home to recuperate.

Repeatedly, I returned to the E.R, a few times because my temperature had spiked and I was dehydrated, until finally, as the chain of events continued, a young concerned physician in the E.R. recommended that I see a gastroenterologist (medical specialists with extensive training in diseases of the digestive tract; equipped to perform tests in making a diagnosis; and to prescribe the best course of treatment to help me recover), and I consider that physician heaven sent (a.k.a. my angel) because after umpteen trips to the E.R. he was finally able to have me admitted into the hospital. And, by the time David escorted me in to his office, I literally couldn't walk, as he wheeled me into the surgeon's office. He examined me and reported that he noticed blood in my stool, and made the decision to admit me, thank God. Finally, I would get the help I needed, instead I progressively got worse.

By the time I was admitted for malaise (general feeling of ill health), my temperature was upwards of 103.3, in addition to not being able to walk, I couldn't feed myself, and felt severe abdominal pain. I was losing weight rapidly because I couldn't eat. No diagnosis could be made because the physicians couldn't determine the cause of my illness. I continued to run elevated temperatures, and was fed liquids through the IV, and wasn't given relief until I was diagnosed with Vasculitis (inflammation of the blood vessels) and possible Polyarteritis Nodosa (PAN), defined by Web MD Health as a rare multi-system disorder that usually becomes apparent between the ages of forty to fifty years, characterized by widespread inflammation, weakening, and degeneration of small- and medium-sized arteries, usually due to disturbances of the body's immune system. What? I didn't have a clue of what Polyarteritis Nodosa meant, but started feeling somewhat better because I was finally able to eat solid foods, and started on steroids (Prednisone) just to bring my temperature down.

However, I'm told, "Mrs. Turner, it appears that your

body is attacking itself for some unknown reason," and of course I'm petrified!

I thought, "What are they talking about? Why would my body be attacking itself?" What are they not telling me? Could it be Aids? Friends were speculating that I might have some other incurable disease. I mean, I heard many different diseases. I wish my dad and my sister Lisa were still living. Is it contagious?

MORPHEA

As I was examined by an array of probing physicians, they all questioned me on the noticeable brown patches covering my thighs. I explained, "I've been diagnosed with an illness called, Morphea (also known as localized Scleroderma; it is a disorder characterized by thickening and indurations of the skin and subcutaneous tissue due to excessive collagen deposition. Morphea subtypes are classified according to their clinical presentation and depth of tissue involvement; they include plaque-type, generalized, linear, and deep varieties. eMedicine2003). A Center City dermatologist (a doctor who specializes in treating diseases of the skin, hair, and nails) diagnosed me after she took a biopsy of the raised brown patches of my skin. She then sent me to another area dermatologist who further determined it to be Scleroderma." I recall that office visit clearly because the physician and I developed a good rapport. We shared a dynamic, enjoyable conversation with the physician asking me a ton of probing personal questions about myself, "Oh how nice, you're married! How many children, lovely, two children, I've never been married myself," and on and on, and I made a mental note of how nice and friendly she was.

However, once she left the room and returned her personality changed into a sinister sounding, "Mr. Hyde" with her reporting bad news! She sort of hissed, "I'm sorry to tell you, you have Scleroderma, goodbye," and then referred me to yet another specialist located in Center City Philadelphia, my very first Rheumatology visit.

SCLERODERMA

I went to a Rheumatologist ("medical doctor who specializes in the diagnosis and treatment of disease at the joints. Rheumatologists may further specialize in diagnosing and treating arthritis and other rheumatic conditions, such as osteoarthritis, rheumatoid arthritis, or lupus.") Web MD. However, before my first office visit I went on-line and goggled Scleroderma on the internet to familiarize myself with my condition and to alleviate some anxiety, but the more I read, the worse I felt. Web MD defines Scleroderma as "a generalized autoimmune disease that causes tightening and thickening of the connective tissue (sclerosis). Systemic sclerosis usually involves the skin, but sometimes it also affects the gastrointestinal tract, the lungs and the kidneys. At the same time a narrowing of the small blood vessels takes place. Because the hardening of the skin is the most typical symptom of the disease, it is called 'Scleroderma.' Since the disease also affects internal organs, the name 'systemic sclerosis' is more precise. The exact cause is unknown, but heredity studies point at the existence of a hereditary susceptibility for the disease, and it mostly develops between the age of forty and fifty." I liked his bedside manner and his reputation as "being tops in his field." In addition, he was extremely positive and encouraging. He said, "That the brown patches which encompassed my thighs were more cosmetic in nature than anything else, and as long as there was no internal organ involvement I need not be alarmed." And, with his professional opinion, I just carried on my life by camouflaging the marks as much as I could. Of course, wearing a bathing suit was out of the question! Luckily, I was already married and my husband was a compassionate man, I bemused!

Several months later, I was admitted in to the hospital, unable to walk or feed myself! Who would've thought? The hospital records dictated that I received two blood transfusions and was "transfused with two units of packed red blood cells," which took a long time to obtain because I had multiple antibodies.

CARDIAC CATHERIZATION AND BIOPSY

My condition began affecting my heart; and attacking the tissue surrounding it, causing my heart to pump only 20%! Wow, this was mind boggling! I was cognizant of my family history of heart disease, especially since Lisa died so young, 37 with coronary artery disease, and I was older than she - 40 years old, and my dad had heart trouble as well. My favorite primary physician, belonged to a team of doctors, Browntree Physicians, was on call that day, and I was glad because she was a very compassionate physician. She was the bearer of this disheartening news, and I couldn't believe my ears, I came in to the hospital to get well, and it seemed I was progressively getting worse! She explained that I would be transported in the morning by an ambulance to another hospital, one that specialized in the heart and when I pressed her for the outcome of heart failure... she said, "more than likely you would require a heart transplant!" She spent a considerable amount of time "holding my hand" and encouraging me that evening. I immediately called David with this unsettling news because he always knows what's best and how to console me. We must have talked for hours, crying together until I was able to sleep with the reassurance that "he would be accompanying me in the morning."

Sure enough, the next morning I was transferred to the Presbyterian Hospital and scheduled for a cardiac catherization to make sure I did not have coronary artery disease, and a heart biopsy (endomyocardial biopsy) to determine whether or not my decreased cardiac function was related to Lupus. And, as I knew he would be, my husband, David was there to make sure everything went according to plan, and to comfort me with his presence.

"A Cardiac Catheterization involves passing a catheter (i.e., a thin flexible tube) through an artery or a vein to the heart, and into a coronary artery. This procedure produces angiograms (i.e., x-ray images) of the coronary arteries and the left ventricle, the heart's main pumping chamber, and also can be used to measure pressures in the pulmonary artery and to monitor heart function, usually in critically ill patients (called right catheterization). In most cases, cardiac catheterization is recommended when a partial or complete arterial blockage is suspected. It is used to evaluate how well the heart is functioning and to obtain information. "

(cardiologychannel.com/cardiaccath/)

"A heart biopsy is done to see what the cells in the heart

muscle look like. The test is most often done after a heart transplant to see if the heart is being rejected by the body. It may also be done if the doctor suspects an infection in the heart, or if the heart is not pumping well for unknown reasons. To do this test, some small pieces of the heart are removed and looked at under a microscope. To get the sample of heart cells, a doctor places a small tube into a large vein in the leg which is then passed into the heart. Some tiny pieces of the heart muscle are removed and sent to the lab where they are carefully examined."

(www.pediheart.org/parents/tests/biopsy.htm)

Fortunately, it was determined negative! Hallelujah! But, I still couldn't walk or feed myself!

Once my temperature was under control, I was released from the hospital. However, they couldn't just send me home because I couldn't walk nor feed myself, and I had lost an excessive amount of weight. In addition, I was left feeling helpless, hopeless and needless to say, very depressed!

Fortunately, one of the hospital's social workers helped to have me placed into Chestnut Hill Rehabilitation Hospital, where I was admitted to regain the use of my hands and mobility skills.

REHABILITATION HOSPITAL

I had a very tough time adjusting to this transition because I had been catered to while in the hospital, the staff took care of my every need, including around the clock assistance (medication, bathroom, dressing, and feeding), and immediately I felt the shift after I was transferred to Chestnut

Hill Rehab. I recall phoning home sobbing uncontrollably." David, I don't like it here! They didn't feed me, no one cares, and I'm uncomfortable, the nurses didn't even come in to greet me when I arrived. I want to come home." David made a few phone calls to the front desk, and immediately a nurse came in to accommodate me. And, as I finished my conversation with her, in walked my husband! Internally, I grinned from ear to ear, and I couldn't help but feel encouraged by the love I felt!

In the beginning of my rehab, I was a very uncooperative patient, partly because I was unaccustomed to my circumstance and was overmedicated. The routine required new patients to attend occupational and physical therapy twice a day, everyday, except weekends. Initially, I felt this schedule was too rigorous for me, even though it was necessary if I didn't want to be crippled and in a wheelchair, depending on others to care for me the rest of my life!

The very first time the attendants came to take me to physical therapy was a challenge for me! I couldn't walk, therefore, they had to roll me onto a machine and then deposit me in to a wheelchair. It was chilling because for forty years prior to this scenario I was "normal" and I could walk just like most everyone else. Luckily for me, one of the nursing attendants charged with my care was someone from the same neighborhood I spent my teenage years in, West Oak Lane, and from that point forward, I felt like a "handicapped queen!" She and her coworkers treated me royally! They were extremely helpful, and encouraged every small step I made or attempted to make! It does help to know someone!

I would attempt to skip some of my early morning

therapy sessions opting to sleep instead, but not there! Staff would send an attendant to bring me down to therapy.

"Get up, Bridget. It's time for therapy. You didn't think you could just not show up, did you? How long is it going to take you to shower?"

After pulling this stunt a few times, I was counseled by the physicians and thought to be suffering from depression and placed on disciplinary probation, and threatened to be kicked out of the rehab. I pulled myself together, because I had no other alternative. Where would I go from here? And what would I do? I couldn't walk, or feed myself properly, and I had to regain my strength in my feet and hands. What other choices did I have?

VISITORS

I was truly embarrassed and didn't want everyone to see me in this condition, but I always had visitors. It seemed, the more uncomfortable I felt about my appearance and the fact I couldn't walk, the more visitors I had. I considered asking people not to come visit because I felt I was looking awful and my vanity started kicking in. Besides, I didn't want to seem too ungrateful, because I loved the support I was getting, but I wished I could look better. I was amazed at the large number of friends and family showing me their love and support. I felt like a celebrity, I received so many flowers, cards, gifts, and telephone calls. Friends called and I still don't remember whether I properly acknowledged everyone formally, but I made the attempt.

INABILITY TO FEED MYSELF

I was devastated and cried daily! One of my most difficult moments at this point, was attempting to use a fork just to eat a meal at rehab in front of my sixteen year old son. Mario. "I can't feed myself," as I sobbed into my three course cafeteria meal, and was totally humbled as one of my biggest cheerleaders fed and cried with me. He was saddened by my defeatist attitude, and encouraged me to try and overcome my lack, for him, both David's, as well as for myself. My sweetie took my illness to heart because it affected him emotionally as well.

BASIC FUNCTIONING

I was an invalid! I had to rely on nurses and nursing assistants to assist me with my basic needs. I couldn't walk, which meant that each time I had to use the bathroom I had to ring the bell for a nursing assistant to help me with a bed pan so that I could urinate or defecate in it as well as wipe my behind! My privacy was out the window! The assistant was also responsible for taking care of my other essentials, like hygiene, sponge washing me so that I would be ready to greet my doctors and visitors smelling fresh, dressing me, usually in a hospital gown, taking my vital signs throughout the day, and assisting me with eating.

However, I recall a time when I wanted to take a shower so badly, but the nursing assistants seemed to be too busy to help me take a shower. Fortunately, my stepmother somehow managed to carry me into that shower, getting soaked in the process. It really is comforting having those who love and care about you in your corner because you'll never know when you'll need someone.

A humbling experience I remember, two of former bosses

Ken Williams and Wayne Morgan visited me in rehab, and the total embarrassment I felt as they saw me confined to a wheelchair. I felt degraded, to say the least! I knew they were feeling extremely empathetic towards me and alarmed by what they saw! "But by the grace of God I am what I am: and his grace which was bestowed upon me was not in vain, but I laboured more abundantly than they all: yet not they not I, but the grace of God which was with me." 1 Corinthians 15:10 (KJV), and just a few weeks prior, I looked as "healthy as a lamb" as I completed my purchasing assignments buying the assortment of supplies I was responsible for obtaining for the company—electrical supplies, appliance parts, stationery, printing, or perhaps metals I bought on a daily basis, and boom... In an instant, I was forever changed. I hated being remembered that way, and I vowed to myself, I had to make a change! I just didn't know how.

I was at the bottom of my rope because I couldn't walk and I didn't know how this could happen and had no clue how to climb out of my predicament! I was feeling afraid, hopeless, dejected, alone, helpless and extremely sorry for myself because I could not get my legs, hands and feet to cooperate! I was discouraged because every doctor assessing my situation seemed to be baffled by my condition.

WHO AM I?

I would be awakened by a nurse or attendant requesting to take my vital signs, heavily sedated and groggy, and filled with many types of new trial medications. Each morning for months my head reeling with confusion/cloudiness from the past night, the chalkboard denoted that I was BRIDGET BOSMANTURNER. I was somebody's wife, married for the second time even, just four years ago in a beautifully celebrated church ceremony to David Turner Jr., and I had children too, but that was in another time and place. I felt as though I were in *The Twilight Zone* television program because my circumstances were so unfathomable.

Why me? "What sort of nightmare am I in? This is a dream and I'm going to wake up."

SYSTEMIC LUPUS ERYTHEMATOSUS DIAGNOSIS

After months of the vague diagnosis of some sort of connective tissue disease, possibly Polyarteritis Nodosa, my Rheumatologist gave me a more definitive diagnosis of Systemic Lupus Erythematosus (SLE). He explained the difficulties in diagnosing Lupus, stating that "there is no single set of symptoms, but a physical exam, and a blood test which can detect a group of antibodies found in the blood of almost all people with SLE." His determination was made because of at least four of the following:

- A compliment test (C_3, C_4, CH_{50}, and CH_{100}) measures the amount of complementary proteins circulating in the blood.

- A sedimentation rate (ESR) or C-reactive protein (CRP) may be used to measure inflammation levels.

- A urine analysis issued to detect kidney problems.

- Chest X-rays may be taken to detect lung damage.

- An EKG can detect heart problems.

I was at once both happy and sad. Happy because finally

the physicians weren't just guessing, and could finally treat my condition accordingly. But sad because my physician couldn't tell me how I acquired Lupus (SLE). However, he stated that there was some genetic involvement. I didn't know very much about Lupus, but what I did know wasn't good! My brother Geneis' friend, Julius, had been diagnosed as a child, and had suffered ever since. My heart always went out to him and his parents because he was constantly in and out of the hospital, his body looked rail thin, and many times I had seen him he appeared to have some open sores, and he appeared very fragile. And, I also remember hearing in the past that Dr. Julius Erving (Dr. J) used to make public announcements on the radio requesting that people support the Lupus Foundation. That was the extent of my knowledge on the topic of Lupus, and now I knew I needed to learn as much as I could about the disease to ensure that I could fight back with a vengeance! Only problem, I was too distraught!

DEPRESSION

My family and friends were visiting me as I muttered, "I'm not going to be in that wheelchair. I'm determined not to be in one! I'm planning to walk," but I wasn't making any strides. I had to be forced to go to therapy

I imagined them saying, "She must be having a breakdown! What a shame! First, Lisa her older sister, (people thought they were twins because they were almost inseparable growing up) died! Then William died (her dad, who took really good care of them both as children)." I was a pitiful sight, down to skin and bones (105 lbs.) as opposed to my pre-sickness weight of 135 lbs., unable to feed or care for myself physically the way I normally had in the past, and lying there ashamed, broken, humbled and feeling sorry for myself, I didn't even recognize who I was in the mirror!

I was an emotional basket case and cried daily because I still couldn't make sense of my situation, frustrated because I didn't know what to expect, and stunned because experienced physicians with their twelve plus years of education couldn't help me. I was disappointed in the healthcare system which I mistakenly expected to save me but I quickly remembered hearing that the only one who could save anyone in this world is the Lord and Savior Jesus Christ!

First order of business, I had to snap out of feeling sorry for myself. Next, as Anthony Robbins says in his tape "Unleash the Power Within," "I had to awaken that sleeping giant within" if only I could open my eyes and stop hiding from this nightmare, my reality, I didn't want to open my eyes! Because of my ignorance I needed to do some research. "My people are destroyed for lack of knowledge: because thou hast rejected knowledge, I will also reject thee, that thou shalt be no priest to me: Seeing thou hast forgotten the law of thy God I will also forget thy children." Hosea 4:6 KJV I was grateful to remember a few key Bible scriptures we were required to recite in Sunday school, and I repeated them over and over in my head. i.e. "Yea, though I walk through the valley of the shadow of death, I will fear no evil: for thou art with me; thy rod and thy staff they comfort me. Thou preparest a table before me in the presence of mine enemies: thou annointest my head with oil; my cup runneth over" (Psalm 23:4, 5).

MUST LEARN EVERYTHING I COULD ABOUT LUPUS

Honestly, I didn't have "a clue" where to begin, so I began my search on the Internet. Systemic Lupus Erythematosus (SLE) as defined by Web MD Arthritis Foundation is "a chronic (long-lasting) rheumatic disease which affects joints, muscles and other parts of the body. Lupus involves inflammation (the immune system's response to kill foreign agents, virus, and bacteria). SLE involves chronic inflammation that can affect many parts of the body, including heart, lungs, skin, joints, blood-forming organs, kidneys and nervous system." According to the Lupus Foundation of America, Southeastern PA Chapter, "Lupus is America's Least Known Major Disease, and was once a fatal disease, but can now be successfully controlled with early diagnosis and treatment."

Because I was in the dark on the subject of Lupus, I began asking the physicians a myriad of questions. *Essence* magazine did a story on Lupus, in which it was reported that, "Lupus affects women during childbearing years," which truly resonated with me because I had given birth to David just three years prior.

I, along with my family and close friends, thought it best that I change physicians to one who was more experienced and on the cutting edge concerning Lupus/Sclerederma cases than the physician I was presently seeing. I was uncomfortable and displeased with my physician because I suffered physically and emotionally under his guidance.

We began asking around and determined that we had the ideal specialist (Rheumatologist), Dr. D. Unfortunately his practice was not accepting new patients because of the heavy demand for his services. Around this same time, I met a young lady named Brigette, my namesake, through her mother, on staff at the hospital, and she was able to convince that very same Rheumatologist to accept me into his practice and override the system. I noticed that Brigette had lost a finger due to Lupus (Raynauds), and she wasn't even uncomfortable with her loss. She didn't even wear a prosthetic. Brigette was a godsend because she was able to help put my disease into remission, through Dr. D, of course.

Brigette and I lost touch, but she remained in my life long enough for the switching of my physician, and to encourage me. I believe it was fate that I met Brigette at all and I am reminded of her each October because we both share the same birth month. What I know for sure is that when God ordains something to happen, it happens at the appointed time!

MY NIGHTMARE CONTINUED

Everything seemed surreal, and I couldn't readily make sense of what was happening to me! It felt as though I were plucked out of my real life just to see what would happen to me! At first, I thought I must have done something extremely wrong for God to be punishing me this way. I remembered as children, we were oftentimes reminded of the wrath God would bestow on us had we been naughty children!

Friends suggested I read the inspirational biblical story of Job, to which I obliged. And, I was better for having read it because as I read about Job's situation I found strength and encouragement for my own predicament especially after I learned that the Lord was aware of what was happening to Job. "All right, do with him as you please, "the Lord said to Satan. "But spare his life." Job 2:6, which indicated to me that Job was never alone, and that the Lord was always with him, as hopefully he is with me, I thought. He lost his possessions, his children, and his health, yet "in all this, Job said nothing wrong "Job 2:10. Job had endured much more than I was going through, but in the end "the Lord blessed Job in the second half of his life even more than in the beginning." (Job 42:12 NLT)

"Testing is difficult, but the result is often a deeper relationship with God. Those who endure the testing of their faith will experience God's great rewards in the end" (Life Application Study Bible, NIV). This study Bible was a gift on my birthday from two of my very close friends, Doris Graham (a bridesmaid in both of my weddings. She became someone I looked up to at work, my mentor, because I wanted to emulate her because she has a very amiable, likeable disposition. While in the hospital she would feed me and read Bible scriptures) and Josephine Hayes, (similar to a family member that you don't always agree with on many issues, yet we love each other just the same. She had been going through emotional life issues herself, she lost her mother, sister and brother, yet she was right there for me. She thoughtfully sent cheerful, hand-written cards to encourage me.). Both, Doris and Josephine are two of my angels who lift me up when I'm down. We always celebrate our birthdays together, and my being in the hospital was no exception. I expressed the desire to have surf and turf, and they brought it to me, yet I was too sick to eat it. But that didn't matter because my family, David, Mario and David III were ravenous that evening, and they enjoyed every morsel!

SPIRITUAL BREAKTHROUGH

One evening during my rehabilitation stay I was feeling the usual sadness and depression all evening. I was sleeping and actually envisioned that there was a battle going on for my soul between God and Satan. I was so frightened that I awoke screaming, causing the nursing attendants to rush in to assess the situation. I was hysterical as I told the nursing staff about my experience/nightmare and how terrified I was and the very next day, the nurse on duty said I kept repeating, "I've got to get out of here, I've got to get out of here!" To calm me down, they moved my bed out into the corridor, in front of the Nurse's Station.

The very next evening, when my friend, Mary Briggs, arrived to visit with me, I informed her of the horrific experience between God and Satan battling for my soul! Without a doubt, the Lord God won the battle as I denounced Satan emotionally pleading with the Lord to deliver me from the grasp of Satan. This experience, confirmed God's love for me because he heard my cries. When no one else could do anything, God who is omnipotent ("having unlimited power or authority; all powerful") and omnipresent ("present in all places at the same time") Webster's New World College Dictionary, fourth Edition, prevailed!

Mary shared that she had been awakened at 4:00 a.m. that very morning and "God instructed her to fast and pray for me." When she spoke to the nurses, they reviewed my chart and said that "I was very disturbed around 4:00 a.m. which caused them to move my bed out of the room to calm me." *"Demons are no match for Jesus so Jesus healed great numbers of sick people who had many different kinds of diseases and he ordered many demons to come out of their victims. But because they knew who he was, he refused to allow the demons to speak" (Mark 1:34).*

TRANSFORMATION

That very next morning, my physician had a staff psychiatrist assess me, and he prescribed some type of psychotic medication. However, the dosage he prescribed turned me in to a zombie and I was unable to function. When I was taken to physical therapy, I would slouch over and fall asleep because of the meds. After a week or so of this psychotic medication, my husband, David, demanded they take me off of them.

Once the psychotic medication was discontinued I became lucid again, and suddenly I was determined to strengthen my legs to walk again. I felt encouraged in my spirit. I believed God would allow me to walk again! I knew it was He who helped me from feeling depressed, and suddenly I was no longer afraid!

Dr. Allyn E. Waller, pastor of Enon Tabernacle Baptist Church in Philadelphia, Pennsylvania, suggests in *Enjoy Your Journey*, "A Christian's life is like a journey" Ecclesiastes 3:1–13 (NKJV). "I know that I am on a journey. And, if I am on a journey, that means God led me this way. And if God led me to this, God will lead me through this. There must be something I needed to learn from it. I can come out with something new that I have learned about God and myself and then I will be ready for the next season of my life." Pastor Waller goes on to suggest, "If you are going to learn your lesson, you have to be present for your promotion. Many of us never move to the next level because we are not present in our pain. You may be looking back, thinking about tomorrow. You are not present in the moment to either feel the pain or enjoy the moment. And then you never move from that moment."

CYTOXAN

Meanwhile, I was readmitted to the hospital from Chestnut Hill Rehab because my temperature had spiked. Apparently, I had inflammation from Lupus which had affected my nerves, causing paralysis in my legs. My Rheumatologist administered Cytoxan (an immunosuppressive medication) intravenously - (IV) pulse therapy. "Immunosuppressive medication, including cytotoxics, which reduce inflammation and suppress the immune system. In higher doses, cytotoxic medications are also used to treat certain forms of cancer. Immunosuppressive medication may be given in pill form, weekly injection, or by intravenous (IV) pulse therapy (injections given monthy. Side Effects may include temporary hair thinning, nausea, and diarrhea." WebMD, Medical Reference from Healthwise.

OH NO, I'M BALD

The nausea and diarrhea were minor in comparison to how horrible I felt I looked when I caught a glimpse of myself in the mirror! I can't say I wasn't forwarned about the probability that I would lose my hair from the Cytoxan treatments or that I had long hair to start, I just didn't expect to look that sick! My cousin, Tine Stone, who feels more like a sister to me than a cousin, came to visit me while I was still in rehab to wash and curl my hair for me, but as she washed and combed my hair, it came out in patches. I was delirious with emotion, "yek, I look so sick, it's going to be embarrassing, I'll have to wear a wig" as I cried hysterically. She empathized with me for a while, but then she stopped, mid-sentence and chastised me, "Okay, Bridget, have a good cry, but then you're going to have to get over it." But, I cried, and cried some more. Meanwhile unbeknown to me, she telephoned her friend and godchild/my previous beauticians (Cynthia and Simone Robinson) and they arrived ready with a wig, scarves, and some freshly blended carrot juice for nutrition. And, fortunately, as Tine hoped it would, the support along with the hair supplies allowed me to gain a better perspective (I am not my hair) and much needed rest.

In the words of Helen Steiner Rice, "The Bend in the Road, Sometimes we come to life's crossroads and view what we think is the end. But God has a much wider vision, and He knows it's only a bend - The road will go on and get smoother, and after we've stopped for a rest. The path that lies hidden beyond us is often the part that is best... So rest and relax and grow stronger—let go and let God share your load, And have faith in a brighter tomorrow—you've just come to a bend in the road."

MUCH NEEDED REST

Staying in the hospital was one of the most isolating times of my life because I felt imprisoned in my own skin. However, it was an excellent time for me to reflect! I felt like I was on a sabbatical from the outside world. All I could do was call on the name of Jesus, day in and day out, crying uncontrollably most days, sobbing to no one in particular, the hospital staff, family and friends as they visited. I wasn't prepared for this nightmare! I felt like I was at the end of my rope, lost and hopeless! This hopelessness went on for months, day in and day out, I felt sorry for myself, refusing to see their recommended shrink or anyone remotely connected to the field of psychiatry. For me, psychiatry was a taboo subject because I considered myself too strong for mental illness. "I was not my parents' child!" I considered myself better than that and too normal for therapy. I remember the attending physician in the hospital scheduled an appointment for me to simply talk to the staff psychiatrist, and when he told me who he was, I went ballistic, even in my deteriorated fragile mental state, exclaiming that "I didn't need to see a psychotherapist because "when I get out of here, I'm planning on becoming a psychotherapist." and with that I refused to discuss my situation with him! Fortunately, they saw past my pride and began administering medication for depression without my consent to stop my constant crying and to help me relax and cope with this major life hurdle. Psychotherapy was going to be my next career field for a few good reasons: 1) Because of my parents conditions and 2) because I consider myself a very good listener and empathizer, and many of my friends/acquaintances seemed to share my viewpoint as they shared their personal lives with me. Several of my friends at work referred to my office as the "Therapists couch" because there was always someone in my chair.

IMPARTING HOPE TO MY CHILDREN

As time progressed one of the physicians on staff, whom I respected and had grown fond of because she seemed to be very caring and genuinely concerned, and who happened to be an Indian, had a heart-to-heart conversation with me and suggested that I begin viewing my situation from my children's sad eyes. She suggested I consider what an impact I was having on them, whether my discouraged mental attitude towards this major life change, along with my failure to make the necessary attempts in therapy day in and day out to help turn my situation around was influencing them and causing them to lose faith and hope. It must have been a combination of timing, my appreciation for her thoughtful bedside manner and her soothing, caring tone that for once in a very long time what she said penetrated and caused me to think about my sons. As if out of a trance, I consciously thought about her question.

Honestly, I was so caught up in how bad I felt, that I had simply never even considered how bad they were feeling, reflecting on countless visits when they asked, "Mom, are you walking yet?" "Mom, can you get up to walk to the bathroom now," and remembering my sixteen-year-old, Mario, literally kicking me in my behind, insisting that I do what I always told him to do, "never give up." As the tears streamed down my cheeks, I felt ashamed of my behavior for not practicing what I had been preaching. For well over 15 years I had been reading all types of self-help, positive mental attitude type books, The Power of Positive Thinking by Norman Vincent Peale, Chicken Soup for the Soul by Jack Canfield, Daily Motivations by Iyanla Vanzant, etc., and I should have been practicing what I had learned, however, because of my inability to walk, all that theory went straight out of the window! The caring Indian physician instrumental in my recovery during rehabilitation suggested that I "at least try to pull myself together and make myself nice for my family on their next visit." There wasn't much I could do to improve my appearance, but at this point a mere smile from me would be a noticeable start. I spruced myself up as best as I could, asking the nursing attendants to assist me, and when my children and husband arrived I consciously focused on their needs, and began for the very first time in a very long time simply asking them about their day, and telling them about my progress so that when they left my rehabilitation room I'm sure they were uplifted, optimistic and hopeful than during their past visits. But more importantly, I had returned from a very long vacation I had taken in my mind and they had their mother/wife back. Walking and turning this humbling situation around for my family became my mission!

MAKE THE CHOICE TO WALK FOR MY SONS: AFTERMATH OF LUPUS DIAGNOSIS
PHYSICAL THERAPY

Finally, after over three months of residing in rehab, attending grueling in-patient physical and occupational therapy two times per day, every day except Sunday where we practiced walking from my assigned wheelchair, the very same wheelchair I was determined not to take home! It was time to go home.

Unfortunately, a major challenge was getting my right foot to cooperate! My right foot had dropped, making it extremely challenging because I had to use my left (stronger) foot to help with the arduously slow task of using the stairs, and when/if that didn't work, I would have to sit down and climb the staircase using my buttocks. After practicing climbing the stairs, I would attempt to walk on a flat surface, walking with a walker, crutches, and finally a cane.

When I went home, my primary therapist suggested that initially I sleep downstairs, camp out on the first floor in the living room to avoid having to climb the stairs. In addition, she suggested I take home a bedpan and a portable toilet to take the pressure off failing and feeling apprehensive about going home.

OCCUPATIONAL THERAPY

In occupational therapy we focused on functioning effectively in our daily lives, practicing new techniques for using our hands in as normal a fashion as reasonably possible, i.e. dressing ourselves, fastening buttons, tying shoe laces, shampooing hair, getting in and off of bed, standing up straight from a chair, lifting a glass to our mouths, cutting our meat, opening up a carton of milk, writing, hygiene issues, like getting on and off the toilet, and taking a shower/bath. In addition, in an attempt to prepare us for going home, we also worked on reach issues, like bending down to pick up things, opening jars which had previously been opened, car doors; conducting errands around the house, like cooking, vacuuming or yard work.

Our homes were made ready for our arrival and handicapped ready to make the transition home as smooth as possible. My bathroom was equipped with a portable shower chair, the shower was adjusted with a spray handle that could be reached while sitting because I couldn't stand without my leg braces in the bathtub because of the muscle weakness incurred, and a portable doughnut for the toilet seat for accessibility. Ready or not, I was released to the loving care of my family, sent home and instructed to follow-up with out-patient therapy!

GOING HOME CRIPPLED

My family couldn't wait to get me home, however, they couldn't care for me because they weren't used to caring for someone who was suddenly crippled! And, of course, I had my concerns! My life had been turned upside down, topsy-turvy from the life I had taken for granted for the past forty years. I didn't want to be a burden! What if I couldn't adapt, or if my family grew tired of my helplessness?

And, just like I expected after I went home, I was even more depressed and miserable than I originally thought possible because of my inability to readily get around! Not being able to walk and hating to use a walker or a cane with assistance made me feel as if I were eighty years old at forty. Feeling like a burden and heavily dependent on others made me feel like a huge disappointment! I hated going to bed because when I had to use the bathroom, I had to ask my husband to escort me, or worse, drag and lift myself up once I finally made it there.

I felt I had come home much too soon because I was literally dependent on my family to do everything for me. Therapy was text book, but I was living real life. Don't get me wrong, naturally, my family was prepared for me at dinnertime or during the day, but after being awakened enough times at 2 AM to assist me in getting to the bathroom would put a strain on anyone, especially when they had to go to work or attend school the next day! To prevent this from occurring, I did my best to not awaken them! I would gently drop myself off the bed, and literally roll and drag myself in to the bathroom, but my efforts were excessively strenuous on me because I still had to return to bed. I wanted my life to return to normal overnight, forgetting that "Rome wasn't built in a day" and I needed to take baby steps. Fortunately, for me, my occupational therapist sent me home with a bedpan!

And, thank God for my family and friends, particularly my late former mother-in-law, Mrs. Bosman, a professionally trained visiting nurse, was up for the challenge of assisting me to recover. Mrs. Bosman was our very own extremely loving drill sergeant who assumed command of my household! She came over my home every single morning for about three months, until she saw to it that I could manage with the assistance of my mother, Geneva. She or my mother would prepare breakfast and lunch for me while, David worked and my boys were in school, and during the evenings David usually made our dinner. In addition, my health plan covered my having a visiting nurse three times per week and she assisted me getting bathed and medicated for the days she was there.

FRANTICALLY SEARCHING FOR A CURE PROPOSED MIRACLE DRUG

Desperately seeking a cure for my condition (disease) because at this point circumstances were looking pretty bleak, a former coworker, Kevin, who knew of my predicament, and that I was sick, walking with a walker, and in need of a miracle, contacted me and told me of a miracle-drug which claimed to help "sick" people cleanse their bodies from impure toxins causing disease, called "Z Greens" (not real name). "Z Greens" was supposed to have been a miracle supplement, a product which a doctor in Germantown was promoting claiming to be excellent for someone like myself. This physician was conducting information sessions in his office in Germantown, so I enlisted my husband and Mary Briggs, to accompany me to his office to test the validity of the product. This African-American physician was alleging that his wife was diagnosed with Lupus and he was allegedly claiming this Z Green product had supposedly improved her condition remarkably.

I'm normally very cynical when it comes to miracle products, but at that point in my life, I was prepared to try most anything. Initially, we were skeptical regarding the benefits of the product, however, what sold me was the testimonial from the wife of the physician discussing her renewed health and strength as well as the credibility and reputation of the doctor.

GALLBLADDER REMOVAL

A week later after I consumed too much of the Z Green product, which I had been faithfully drinking, I was so sick, I was re-admitted to Chestnut Hill Hospital with intense unbearable stomach pangs from 6/12/02–6/16/02 suffering from epigastric abdominal pain, and instead of me getting better, I was in constant pain, and diagnosed with Acute Cholecystitis (gallbladder). I ended up having my gallbladder removed immediately, called a Laparoscopic Cholecstectomy. It was questionable whether "Z Greens" was the cause of my gallbladder being removed, but I stopped taking the concoction immediately. In fact, I threw the product in the trash and started not returning Kevin's calls until I decided to express how I felt regarding the product, and to his credit, he had no knowledge of any adverse effects of Z Greens. After our conversation, he discontinued attempting to convince me of my need for the product any further.

LEFT FLANK PAIN

Once again, I was readmitted to Chestnut Hill Hospital from 7/4/02–7/12/02 for left flank pain and rescheduled for a Cystoscopy (test that allows the doctor to look at the interior lining of the bladder and the urethra). The doctor examines the inside of the bladder for stones, tumors, bleeding, and infection and the results were negative

TRANSITIONAL CARE UNIT OF CHESTNUT HILL

BILATERAL LEG BRACES

I was depressed, and hated attempting to get out of bed because without assistance I would fall flat on my face. I was assigned yet another physical therapist, but this one seemed different, and extremely caring, and she had a wonderful idea to get me out of bed and moving around. She suggested bilateral ankle braces she had first seen demonstrated elsewhere, and, of course, I didn't have any idea how braces would get me moving because I felt so vulnerable and helpless.

Initially, they were extremely awkward and clunky, however, my physical therapist was determined to make me a successful case, as she completed her graduate studies in therapy, making me her thesis. She was in my hospital room more than I was. She worked around my pill schedule, and little by little she would show up.

"Bridget, would you like me to come back after you've showered, or eaten, or at a better time?"

Gradually, I gave in and stopped resisting her caring requests that I "at least try to walk in them" and, eventually, I could walk, even if it were with assistance! She would show up every day and coach me, as I took baby steps, holding on to the walls, while the nurses and aids at Chestnut Hill clapped and encouraged me with their smiles and kind words of enthusiasm.

Eventually, I could walk to the bathroom unassisted, and it was a remarkable feeling! I didn't have to ring the bell for the nursing attendant to bring me a "dreaded bed pan as I made an embarassing bowel movement in it." Yes, those braces were a godsend because I felt helpless and embarrassed lying in the bed as my children, friends, relatives, and husband visited!

At night, when I had to go to the bathroom, I would ring the bell for assistance to get in to my braces, and I began feeling humiliated, so I slept in them, until the nurses instructed me to "take them off while I slept to give my legs a rest and not cause more circulation difficulties."

This time when I was discharged home, I had a new found freedom! I could get up at night and roam my home without waking up my husband. What a blessing. Leg mobility is definitely taken for granted. It's like catching the bus when you've been used to driving a car. Kiss those legs, and thank God for them. "I can do all things through Christ which strengthens me" (Philippians 4:13 KJV).

OUTPATIENT THERAPY

My legs were discouraging for me to look at! They appeared skinny, decrepit, with brown scaly, ugly dead skin all over my calves from total disuse. It seemed that my legs were disconnected from my body as it was evident that I was very uncomfortable touching them! Initially, David, who had been given family leave privileges, would accompany me to outpatient therapy sessions because I couldn't drive and to get me acclimated to the routine of therapy. I was assigned an extremely, knowledgeable and caring outpatient physical therapist named Charlotte. Charlotte appeared to feel sorry for me, and I believe she thought I would never walk!

Therapy was tough, but Charlotte was even tougher on me because she pushed me to my limits to try using and strengthening my muscles. She worked out various routines that seemed redundant and sometimes rather silly and ineffective to me, like placing a ball between my legs and holding it in place or standing in place while holding onto the bed. I must admit that initially I was a skeptic regarding therapy because before this major downfall I wasn't even aware of the benefits of this type of service of rebuilding lives. I sometimes mistakenly thought Charlotte concocted routines to try to keep me occupied while she assisted some other patient on some exercise apparatus. There were numerous people in addition to me working with other therapists, athletes who incurred injuries, people who may have lost a leg and were working on balance, MS patients, etc. However, over time, gradually we both started witnessing great improvement and I now am a testament to the power of therapy!

Months later, I developed more and more confidence,

and I grew antsy enough to begin driving again! After all I had a new silver Toyota Avalon parked in front of the house just waiting to be driven by me ... not my sixteen year old, Mario, who had been discovered by my husband, David, sneaking and driving my car all the while I was sick and in the hospital. I remember, I was scheduled for surgery and David called to inform me that my car was missing! I told him to report it stolen to the police, but after a little investigation on his part, he contacted Mario at Saul High School to find out whether he had taken the car to school? Yes, he replied, "I have the car!" Sixteen years old with no license and no permit! Needless to say, David retrieved my car and they key, and Mario was forbidden to drive it until he obtained his credentials! As I was saying, months later, I developed enough confidence to begin venturing to drive.

By this time, David had to return to work on a routine basis, leaving me stranded during the day. I felt I had no other choice - I took the chance, while wearing my leg braces driving myself to my therapy appointments, accompanied by my mother for support. Granted, my mother has a license, and can drive, but because of her insecurity driving, I would drive us to therapy, and then as a reward we would go to lunch and take in a movie. Driving became my therapy. Gradually, I began making lunch dates with co-workers, and fellow therapy patients.

VACATIONS

The ultimate challenge for me was planning and scheduling two terrific family vacations while still wearing leg braces. Once I thought I could, my family and I were off to Disney World, Florida. At the last minute, David couldn't accompany us on our departure because of work constraints, which was somewhat unsettling at first, but Mario, who was now seventeen years old, and whom we always considered an old soul, knew exactly how to handle my limitations. At the airport and in the theme park in Florida, he quickly located wheelchairs and pushed me around with David III, who was four years old, resting on my lap. My children and I bonded because of the experience, and in actuality, we discovered the perks of my being in a wheelchair, i.e. we were ushered to the front of every line we were in at the airport as well as the theme parks. We saw Beauty and the Beast, Indiana Jones, toured EPCOT, etc. In addition, we also vacationed in Ocean City, Maryland, and stayed in one of their luxury condominiums, where I was able to get some clarity while relaxing, reading, and writing, as our family spent that glorious time together.

CHALLENGES OF PILL REGIMEN
REMEMBERING TO TAKE THEM

Because of my diagnosis (SLE, Sclerederma and Raynaud's *Phenomenon), I must t*ake a variety of medication including steroids, Plaquenil, and Neurontin, as well as a variety of vitamins daily including multi-vitamins, calcium, flaxseed oil, and baby aspirin, to keep my illness under control. In all honesty, it feels like a job, as I am required to take medication four times per day! In the hospitals, administering medication is part of the responsibility of the registered nurses (RN's), not the assistants or the licensed general practitioners (LGPN's).

At times, it's difficult to remember to take my required medicine, especially, if I'm preoccupied doing something else. However, my body quickly reminds me, and I quickly take the forgotten pills. For example, when I don't take Neurontin, I experience stiffness and have difficulty getting out of bed.

REMEMBERING TO RE-ORDER FROM MAIL ORDER PHARMACY

To save on costs, my employer requires us to use a mail order pharmacy for refilling maintenance medication, and if I so happen to run out, which has happened on occasion, it's a nightmare because I can't simply go to the local pharmacy to ask for a refill. Unfortunately, it takes fourteen days from the time of request to be filled. Needless to say, it is advantageous to keep an adequate supply.

BENEFITS TO HAVING A EMPLOYER PRESCRIPTION PLAN

However, because I worked twenty-two years, I am very fortunate to have a prescription plan provided by my employer because my pills only cost me five to ten dollars maximum. Whereas, my mother, who never worked anywhere for long, doesn't have a prescription plan and her medication runs as high as one hundred plus dollars,

DISABILITY INSURANCE

MEDICATION REGIMEN

As a teenager realizing my dad had to take quite a bit of prescription medication to keep him functioning well, I sometimes wondered why, but I thought, if that's what keeps my dad healthy, so be it! That's life! But, I used to be so very thankful that I didn't have to take medication myself. But, my how times have changed!

I reflect on our conversations about disability and disability insurance, and as the saying goes, "Father does know what's best!" "Bridget, listen to me, you're young and healthy, and now's the time to purchase disability insurance because once you're sick or diagnosed with an illness, carriers won't insure you. Your bad health will follow you because insurers run tests on their insured and many times poll their physicians to make certain you are indeed healthy and a good risk."

And, of course, being the know-it-all young adult, I'd retort, "I don't need disability insurance because one, it costs way too much, two, I don't plan on getting sick, and three, my employer has disability insurance."

We would continue to have our father/daughter pep talks over time, and he would always ask that proverbial question. "Have you purchased that insurance I told you about yet?"

I would counter with, "No, because I didn't know who to call."

Eventually, he began sharing the names of some insurance carriers... and finally, it wasn't until after he really started opening up and "disclosing personal details about himself, that he also carried disability insurance and provided me with the names of his company or a company he had used in the past, along with an agent to directly contact," that I seriously began to listen.

I listened intently because I admired and respected my dad because he pulled himself up from when I remembered him having a nervous breakdown, losing our home on Temple Road, purchasing a new single home, remarrying and always keeping new vehicles, and having a seemingly un-endless cash and credit flow. I was so proud to say he was my dad!

Daddy insisted that I figure out how much money I was living off of per month, and purchase that amount of insurance. At the time we thought $2,000 per month of insurance would cost me $43, and was a small amount to pay, especially if I ever became disabled.

Needless to say, after consulting with an agent, and submitting to their vigorous physical exam (urine analysis, blood tests, etc.), when my health was great, approximately 34 or 35 years of age, I purchased disability insurance, and when I told my dad he lit up with joy that I finally heeded his advice. However, several years later, after my policy increased an additional $20 per month, I attempted to cancel my coverage because I didn't think I could afford it.

Thus, I looked for ways to cut back and tighten my budget. I was forever robbing Peter to pay Paul. And after a discussion with a buddy who thought I'd benefit more if I deposited the money I was paying for disability insurance in to my bank account.

Fortunately, the insurance carrier hadn't acknowledged my request to discontinue coverage before I applied for my claim.

And, if my dad were alive today, he would say, "Didn't I

tell you, you don't listen to your pop." His wisdom was not wasted on me because I listened and every month when I cash my check, I thank my daddy.

RHEUMATOLOGY NIGHTMARE

When I returned from vacation in the Virgin Islands, I immediately made an emergency appointment to see my Rheumatologist, Dr. Jones (not his real name) because "I couldn't stop a burning sensation which was pulsating in my fingertips." Dr. Jones wasn't even alarmed he simply prescribed something to ease the pain.

However, the burning sensation persisted and I ended up back in his office several times, until finally, David accompanied me to his office because we were seriously getting concerned because I had been taking huge amounts of pain medication just to allow the pain to ease up enough for me to sleep at night! We expressed our concern, and David pointed out that from his experience of being in the United States Air Force they were trained to identify problems, and to him "it looks like Bridget's fingers have been frostbitten, sort of like gangrene." However, the supposed knowledgeable doctor, disagreed, prescribed Lovenox, which I was required to inject into my stomach, a process I never thought I could do, but I did it because I had faith in the Rheumatologist. Meanwhile, my fingers were growing more and more discolored, and the pain was unbearable until finally, I could not take the pain any longer.

PRIMARY CARE PHYSICIAN

It was during the afternoon, while David III, who was three

at the time, and I were at home watching "Teletubbies" when the burning in my fingers became enraged and I couldn't take it any longer! I grabbed David, put him in the car, and I drove hysterically to my Primary Care Physicians (Browntree Associates) not their real name, and demanded that I see my doctor because the pain in my fingers wouldn't stop! I was beside myself, crying uncontrollably, as my poor baby, David, looked on helplessly!

The physician directed me to go straight to Chestnut Hill E.R. and she called to tell them to expect me! I called my husband to come pick up baby David, and I drove to the hospital. There I was given more pain medication, and transferred to the hospital affiliated with my Rheumatologist, and it was there that I was informed that I had what my husband had predicted, "gangrene."

I dropped that Rheumatologist in a heartbeat after I discovered just how incompetent/inexperienced he really was, and went with a seasoned professional. I learned a valuable lesson in sticking with someone who is just starting out!

DROPPED BY BROWNTREE
(PRIMARY CARE PHYSICIAN)

After I endured the fingertip trauma, And, right there in the middle of my agony, I was dropped from their practice and directed to find another physician more experienced in dealing with complex Lupus cases. I was devastated! What next.

DARKNESS

FEAR   PAIN

CONFUSION

SADNESS

LOST

SECRETS

QUIET

ANGER

HIDING

CHAPTER XX
_____

LOSS OF THREE FINGERTIPS —
REPULSION AND SHAME
(2003)

July 2003 I poured everything into planning my Mom's sixtieth birthday party, and it was an overwhelming success, except that I wished Lisa were alive to share in the joy! Most of our relatives and a few of her friends were there, Uncle Lewis Stone, Aunt Dolly Huff, and practically everyone I had invited. David barbequed for the festivities, and my children, Mario and David, and especially my Mom had a fantastic time, and I'm snapped back to reality, as the lanky be-speckled physician with the German accent sails into the sterile white hospital room and diagnoses' my fate.

"Mrs. Turner, it looks as though you have gangrene in your fingertips, and unfortunately we'll need to amputate in order to keep the gangrene from spreading!"

"What? No! You're not going to cut my fingers off. What's gangrene? How did I get black necrotic fingertips?"

"Gangrene is tissue death, apparently, you lost blood flow to the tips of your fingers due to your illness, Raynaud's Phenomenon related to Lupus." Raynaud's phenomenon, as defined by Web MD NIAMS (National Institute of Arthritis and Musculoskeletal and Skin Diseases) "is a disorder that affects the blood vessels in the fingers, toes, ears, and nose. This disorder is characterized by episodic attacks, called vasospastic attacks that cause the blood vessels in the digits (fingers and toes) to constrict (narrow). Raynaud's phenomenon can occur on its own, or it can be secondary to another condition such as Scleroderma or Lupus."

"Close to 90% Lupus Erythematosus and Sclerederma patients experience Raynaud's attacks, and are most commonly triggered by cold, through emotional upset, the use of vibrating tools and certain drugs (including caffeine and cigarettes) can also do this. Though not normally serious, if it is severe, prolonged or frequent ischemia (lack of supply) will cause damage, scarring or even loss of tissue. In rare instances gangrene may develop. The impaired blood supply also predisposes to infection, ulceration and poor healing of minor cuts and abrasions" (eLupus.com Emerge into Wellness).

"I can't imagine living or even wanting to live with no fingers."

"Mrs. Turner, we won't need to take off much, just the part that's necrotic, (black in color), and causing the pain! If we don't remove the dead tissue, it'll spread and you could end up losing your entire hand. Besides, some prosthetics are designed now where you can't tell the difference. I'll even leave you part of your fingernails which looks like it hasn't been infected." I turn my head away as the tears stream down my cheeks.

Sobbing quietly, I nod my head up and down, and reluctantly respond, "Okay." Thinking back, when did I first notice there was something wrong with my fingers? I was on vacation in St. Thomas with a few of my traveling friends, Doris Graham and Josephine Hayes, and we were dining at a poolside buffet which included spicy fish and wings I had only recently enjoyed eating when all of a sudden I began experiencing a fiery hot burning sensation in the tips of my fingers. Because I had been eating with my fingers, I thought possibly that the seasoning was causing the burning sensation, so I washed my hands. But, when that didn't work, I took the prescribed pain medicine, either Dalaudid or Percocet to help soothe the discomfort.

The very first operation to rid my hand of this horrifying black invasion, gangrene, was a total failure, and my pain level tripled! The hospital kept me heavily sedated, and to my surprise, a few days later discharged me into the care of the hand surgeon who had performed the surgery's care, with a prescription for an ample supply of pain killers. I believe they prescribed Darvocet, which I devoured. However, I continued to feel excruciating pain!

I was alarmed that this physician had performed surgery on me, but I was still experiencing so much pain! For weeks following the surgery I was on an emotional roller coaster! I cried and complained, couldn't eat, wouldn't bathe, and found it difficult to rest. At night I tossed and turned, and made it extremely difficult for anyone in the house to sleep, especially my husband, who is a light sleeper. I tried to escape my pain by moving in to our youngest son's bedroom for privacy. I was in pure agony and shared my distress with my family. I exclaimed non-stop, "My fingers hurt, and they feel like they're on fire." It was a trying time in our household because the pain was so intense and unbearable! A week or so later, I had a follow-up at my hand surgeon's office, accompanied by my spouse, David, son, Mario, as well as my mother, Geneva. All three escorted me for support because I was a basket case and the hand surgeon's explanation of the surgery was that he hadn't taken off all the gangrene, and would have to operate again, and as he explained he seemed very detached and cold after the surgery. He spoke to me as if he had no compassion for the pain I was in. He seemed aloof and egotistical, as if he couldn't believe his surgery was a failure. But then I was the one who asked him to leave as much of my nail as possible, didn't I?

OH NO, GANGRENE DETECTED IN FOOT—CIRCULATOR BOOT THERAPY—DISTRESSED

During this same hospitalization, I had an ingrown nail, or so I thought. I informed the attending physician, and he diagnosed it as "nothing more than a blood blister." He popped it with a sterilized needle and covered it with a bandage. A few weeks later when the bandage was removed, my toe was "black" just like my fingertips were. The hospital's podiatrist took one look at my toe and decided to amputate! He asked me to sign a form granting him authority to amputate "possibly just my toe, but it could involve my foot, or even my leg. I was livid and refused to give my signature! First, my fingers and now my toe, and I couldn't imagine having both cut at the same time!

    Fortunately, there was a surgeon familiar with an alternative procedure called "the Circulator Boot." The Circulator

Boot treats circulation problems ranging from micro dysfunction (arterial and venous shunting) small and large arterial vessel disease and venous pathology. The Circulator Boot controls infection due to the secondary function that includes an enclosed bag system of electrolyte and antibiotic solutions pumped into the wounds. Aggressive debridement to clean the wound stimulates some active bleeding. The difficult task was going to the Wound Center three times per week. Almost within a month, we all started to see improvement. The granulation had already started. The end result was that I totally healed within four months, and I only lost a piece of my toe, as opposed to much more, and for that I am extremely grateful.

HAND THERAPIST

The next step was for me to meet my hand therapist, Carla. I cried hysterically when I made my first office entrance, and it took my husband, mother and son to accompany me. When I arrived, I hooped and hollered because I couldn't control the lightning that was flashing inside my opened wounded fingers! "Throbbing, Throbbing, Throbbing." Everything was a blur and all I could do was cry and pray. I'm certain I looked like a basket case, but I couldn't escape the pain I was in, and everyone I encountered in that mental state seemed to empathize with me and have some type of suggestion, but nothing worked.

Unfortunately, Carla was only able to advise me, "Bridget, you must contact your primary care physician or your Rheumatologist because Dr. Hand Surgeon cannot prescribe anything. Would you like to lie down?"

I must have looked and smelled horrible, but I didn't

care how bad I smelled because I was in excruciating pain. I remember not even brushing my teeth because I was trying to arrive at my appointment on time to seek relief from my misery.

"My poor hand. I earned my living using my fingers and now my hand looks deformed. I'm embarrassed, and I don't want anyone to see them, especially my son, David III. I don't want him thinking Mommy looks ugly or bad in any kind of way. I kept asking for pain medication, anything, Davrocet, Oxycontin, Percocet.

My family, especially my husband was getting worried because I wasn't showering or bathing the way I normally had in the past. In fact, I was sleeping in my clothes and popping pain pills left and right, and no one in our house was getting any sleep because I cried and whined all night like an alley cat.

Because I couldn't sleep at night I would sleep in David III's bedroom so my husband could try and rest for work the next day. As I would cry into his pillow, my older son, Mario, would enter the room and curl up right next to me and attempt to encourage me, and he would say, "Mommy, try to be strong, and not give up. Imagine I'm your coach. Sometimes you have to feel the pain," because I would be crying and praying to die. But then he'd be telling me he didn't want to live without me, and I'd try to muster the strength to get through the nights.

Well, hand therapy continued for well over a month with my alternating seeing the doctor, and attending hand therapy where the therapist would carefully unwrap the bandaged hand, of which I couldn't bare to look at, and place gauze on the wounds, insert my hand in their sterilized whirlpool, massage it, and instruct me on exercising it.

This routine was great, but my fingertips were still black and I was still in excruciating pain, and on vast amounts of prescription pain medication. The pain was so intense that I was becoming a regular outpatient at Chestnut Hill and Bryn Mawr Hospital emergency rooms, where they would kindly discharge me back home with a new prescription for pain and suggest that I "see my physician." I was beginning to lose faith in doctors and hospitals, and really believing more and more in God bringing me through.

For some unknown reason, the pain would subside somewhat during the day, but at night, watch out, because I'd be up howling like a coyote, and my husband would be uttering something about him having to go to work the next day! On one such night, I just couldn't take the intensity of the pain a night longer! I had endured too much, and I was sick and tired of my husband telling me "simply to sleep." If I could sleep I would!

Forget him, I thought. *What does he know about my pain?* The pain and discomfort was going to end this night!

UNBEARABLE PAIN

I threw myself down the steps and proceeded to take myself to somebody's emergency room, but with one problem! I was restricted from driving, my throbbing gangrenous hand was still bandaged and I was too doped up, and in so much pain that at this point I would have probably crashed if I attempted to drive. Nevertheless, I was on my way, but Mario was there to catch my fall! I love that sweetheart! Did I raise him? Oh yeah, I did.

He drove me to the hospital and because I couldn't make the emergency physicians take me seriously because I was a repeat emergency room patient, I devised a story to get them to do something about my distress. I told them I was crazy and seeing things. Fortunately, one of the kind-hearted physicians saw right through what I was telling him, and I admitted the real reason for my visit as he unwrapped my raw, black bandaged hand. He knew I was telling the truth, and made a recommendation that I return to the hand surgeon.

At this point, I couldn't stomach the hand surgeon who had originally operated on me because he should have done something about this pain, so I decided to search for another hand surgeon, and fortunately he decided to get rid of the entire fingernail, once and for all. Guess what? These guys were partners, but the latter one's bedside manner was much more down to earth and empathetic.

I remember, it was a Saturday morning, and this same inconsiderate physician made an off-handed cavalier remark, "What are you anxious about, it won't happen over the weekend!" I was so upset that I called my friend/confidant, Mary Briggs, and she helped to ease my distress. She calmed me down and said she was coming to the hospital. When she hung up from me she said she immediately went into prayer and God led her to a sermon one of her ministers, Rev. Blocker, had previously preached on with a sermon text of "What do you do when you don't know what to do." The scripture text was Philippians 4:6–8. "Don't worry about anything; instead pray about everything. Tell God what you need and thank him for all he has done. If you do this, you will experience God's peace, which is far more wonderful than the human mind can understand. His peace will guard your hearts and minds as you live in Christ Jesus" (Philippians 4:6–8 NLT).

When she arrived I was reading the exact same scripture! Remarkably, when Mary arrived, she noted that I was sitting there trying to recite that same scripture her minister had preached on. She said, "You were trying to memorize it because you were repeating parts of it with your eyes closed."

FINAL AMPUTATION

After my three fingers were amputated at the nail and all the blackness was destroyed forever, I sunk deeper into a hole of self-pity. All I could imagine was how bad I would look to others, including my husband, children and myself! I was glad they were bandaged and when the therapist changed the dressings I couldn't bear to look. I was disgusted with how grotesque I felt. I felt sick to my stomach every time I tried to look at them. I wondered whether my husband would even want me missing part of my limbs, if my children would feel ashamed that I was their mother deformed, and embarrassed because of my newfound disability, and wondered whether I would be able to function with my right hand ever again.

I remember Mrs. Bosman used to come over to take care of me, and because she had one of her legs amputated because of sugar diabetes, she could relate to what I was feeling. I had worked myself into a tizzy fit, crying and feeling ashamed about the loss of my tips, she removed her prosthesis, even though I couldn't bring myself to look, but she insisted forcing me to take a glimpse. She left me with these words, "Bridge, you are not your fingers, if I can live without my leg, I'm sure you can live without your fingers." In retrospect, Mrs. Bosman wore her artificial leg for many years, but never once had she removed it. But at this difficult time in an attempt to help me overcome my shame, she thoughtfully whipped that leg off, chose to open up and reveal the part of herself she seemed to be most uncomfortable about.

After months of progressive hand therapy, I still became embarrassed when others including my family and friends, saw my mangled hand. I constantly inquired as to when I would be able to be fitted for my hand prostheses, and I was always told "it's too soon...."

And, finally, it wasn't until I was fitted for my prostheses that I felt like I had my hand and life back.

HAND PROSTHESES

To my knowledge, there are only a few manufacturers of hand prostheses in the metropolitan area. I had my first set of digital prostheses made for me by a well known out-of-network prosthetic company located in New York City because they came very highly recommended by my hand surgeon who was very familiar with the quality of their craftsmanship, but because they were an out-of-network provider my health insurance carrier would not cover the entire cost of manufacturing, therefore, I had to pay a hefty deductible just to regain a portion of my self-confidence. Unfortunately, they are very fragile, became damaged, and needed replacing all too soon. I applied for a second set, but received a rejection from the insurance company because they have a shelf-life of at least three years. Determined to get a replacement set, a month later I appealed their decision, and after presenting my case in their downtown boardroom to their Review Committee, discussing the true need for their wear, and showing the defective condition they were in, I was cleared to order my second set.

Unfortunately, the process for manufacturing is extremely lengthy. In the interim, I either wrap my fingers or wear band aids to hold the prostheses in position because I require them to work, drive my car, type and to hold an ink pen. In addition, I am right-handed and because I am accustomed to wearing them to detract from people staring and to avoid feeling self-conscious.

But, this time, I opted to go with an in-area network Philadelphia supplier that sub-contracted out to a Maryland manufacturer because I rationalized that if the out-of-network supplier was so fantastic, why didn't they last and why pay another deductible for something that didn't last in the past from the same supplier?

Both companies create authentic looking digital prostheses constructed of silicone, restore the length for functional use like writing and typing, balance the hand and provide aesthetics for psychological, professional and social benefits. I enjoy showing people my hand because I enjoy watching the surprised look on their faces as they look on in total disbelief, including physicians, who often comment "they've never seen anything quite like them."

TREATMENT FOR RAYNAUD'S PHENOMENON

Take action during an attack! Condition cannot be cured, but it can be managed as follows, according to Web MD eLups.com Emerge into Wellness.

- Avoid severe cold or dramatic changes in temperatures. Wear gloves if the outside temperature is down.

- Keep your whole body warm.
- Don't smoke.
- Reduce consumption of coffee, tea or other caffeinated drinks.
- Exercise regularly to maximize blood flow.
- Keep stress at bay: get involved in meditation or mindfulness practices.
- Pay attention to small cuts and abrasions so that they don't become infected. Get treatment if infection occurs.
- Check if medications (prescribed or otherwise) might aggravate Raynauds.
- Reduce severity of attacks by warming hands (e.g. in warm water).

If serious, see physician. There are medications that can help Raynauds.

- Radial Sympathectomy
- Prostaglandins and Alprostadil
- Cialis and Viagra

ALPROSTADIL

It helps that my current physician is aware of my underlying condition, Raynaud's Phenomenon, because Dr. D. is able to administer the latest research for treating Lupus. I was extremely concerned! My fingers were blue and on their way to completely losing blood flow, but because we're aware of my underlying condition (Raynaud's Phenomenon), I went for treatment, which I believe saved my fingers. .

Dr, D admitted me into the hospital where I received the medicine intravenously. . "Alprostadil is a type of medicine that causes blood vessels to expand, increasing blood flow throughout the body. It can be given either by injection or as a suppository". (Web MD Medical reference provided in collaboration with the Cleveland Clinic)

CIALIS AND VIAGRA

My physician has also begun using Cialis or Viagra, male erectile dysfunction medication, on me because of their effectiveness in causing the blood to flow throughout the female's body as well. (Web MD)

REVATIO

A drug called Revatio may help treat an aggressive condition called pulmonary arterial hypertension. Revatio has the same active ingredient - Sildenafil—as Viagra.

(Web MD)

"I have plenty to boast about and would be no fool in doing it, because I would be telling the truth. But I won't do it. I don't want anyone to think more highly of me than what they can actually see in my life and my message, even though I have received wonderful revelations from God. But to keep me from getting puffed up, I was given a thorn in my flesh, a messenger from Satan to torment me and keep me from getting proud.

Three different times I begged the Lord to take it away.

Each time he said, "My gracious favor is all you need. My power works best in your weakness." So now I am glad to boast about my weaknesses, so that the power of Christ may work through me. Since I know it is all for Christ's good, I am quite content with my weaknesses and with insults, hardships, persecutions, and calamities. For when I am weak, then I am strong "(2 Corinthians 12:6–10).

DARKNESS

FEAR   PAIN

CONFUSION

SADNESS

LOST

SECRETS

QUIET

ANGER

HIDING

FUTHER LOSSES

CHAPTER XXI

MARY ELAINE BOSMAN

(2005)

On April 20, 2005, Mary Elaine Bosman, my ex-husband's mother, passed away, but her spirit remains, like that of my sister and father, in my heart. She was the mother I needed, during many crucial times in my life when mom wasn't available because of moments of her mental health issues, and when I was just seventeen years old, and in love with her son Mario, she taught me to take care of myself physically.

She would say, "Bridge, never suffer with a headache when you can take an aspirin." When I was yet maturing and most of my hair fell out, she helped to care for it and grow it back by massaging my temples, and washing and curling it until it returned.

When I started my first job and spoke too rapidly to be understood, she was the one who called me and encouraged me to practice answering the phone slowly, all the while encouraging me to improve. She believed in me until I began believing in myself. She would say, "Go head, girl, you're going to be featured in *Essence* or *Jet* one of these days."

When I was in the hospital and feeling all alone, sad and blue, I would look up like a frightened child and she would be there to hold my hand and to tell me everything would be okay, and I trusted what she said was true because I believed in her.

When I went home from the hospital she nursed me back to health in spite of the fact that her health was failing. She had diabetes and had her own leg amputated years back, and when I learned I would also have to lose three fingertips, she was instrumental in helping me to cope! I remember in my blue funk, she took off her prosthetic leg and made me look at it, and come to grips with my reality. And, when I resisted taking Plaquenil, for fear of the stigma attached to taking them and possibly becoming addicted. We had long discussions on the need to take them vs. the need not to until she finally convinced me, just like her aspirin analogy she used on me, "Why suffer when I could get relief." Mrs. Bosman was one of my biggest cheerleaders, and I know she would be so proud of my book today because as I moped around doing nothing in particular, feeling hopeless she would sweetly say, "Have you been on your computer yet?" There was one particular song she said which played in her mind and helped her always continue to persevere in life, and she searched high and low for that song, and she would not rest until she located a copy of it. She purchased a copy of that song entitled "You Can Make It" in a distant record shop just before she went to be with the Lord.

MARCH 2005 – LOSING LEXIS

We had a beautiful, brown and white full bred Shetland Sheep dog that Mario named Lexis. She was a gentle, mild-mannered dog that resembled a miniature Lassie (collie). We loved her because she was like another member of our family. We had her as a puppy for twelve glorious years, and I never knew I could love an animal as if she were my very own child. After Mario Corvette and I were divorced, when Mario was seven, Lexis was purchased as a companion for him by his dad. However, when he became a teenager, he grew tired of the responsibilities of caring for her, and she became my responsibility. I used to walk her when the weather permitted. However, if it was too chilly or I was too tired, I would let her out, and she would return after exploring our neighborhood.

Unfortunately, I let her out on March 16, 2005 because it was too cold, and I fell asleep, and that was the last time we saw her! Somehow she never returned! We searched for her, and even offered a reward for her return, posting flyers, asking neighbors, etc. but she never returned. We guessed that someone may have taken her because she was a full bred, beautiful, and smart!

We enjoyed many wonderful moments with her, especially each time I returned home from the hospital, Lexis would cuddle up to me, as if she sensed I was hurting, and nurse me back to health. I would fall asleep, and wake up next to Lexis. Unfortunately, she's gone forever, but I'll always remember she taught me to love a dog unconditionally! One day we'll purchase another dog, and hopefully she'll be as special as Lexis!

WHAT'S NEXT?

CASINO GAMBLING — POOR STEWARD

I gambled as a diversion after I retired from my career because I wasn't happy. I missed going to work, had excessive idle time and you know the saying, "an idle mind is the devil's workshop," and boy did I play. My husband's style is laid back; therefore, I had extensive autonomy, and because my mother could cover for me with David III. Initially, I gambled for excitement and fun, but soon it became a challenge to see if I could win against the casinos and to win extra money to buy casino memorabilia, but in the process I became consumed with receiving money quickly to purchase things money could buy.

I planned the most disastrous family vacation to Las Vegas, Nevada and our nightmare began. Actually, it was Mario's twentieth birthday and we dined at the famous Wolfgang Puck's fabulous restaurant and had a so-so experience. The wings were really tasty, but for our younger folks, they would have enjoyed burgers and fries from some fast food restaurant, but overall we enjoyed the experience. Mario excused himself and went to our celebrity suite and his friend naturally followed, while David took David, III to the game room, and that left me to myself to have a good time, and I chose to gamble, and I played the $10 black jack table and tried to win money, enough to take us all to the "O" Show or to the Grand Canyon because David III wanted to see it. I asked the dealers and fellow players about the cost, and I heard $250 per person. I played to win, but I lost! I lost big time!

I returned to the room to tell my husband I had lost all the money I brought on vacation, and he hit the ceiling!

"You lost two thousand dollars, you Idiot! How could you lose all your money gambling? We can't do anything now."

It was crazy! Just as crazy as carrying credit card debt totaling over $25,000 to $45,000 with interest rates over 19%! But, I'm guilty of both. It would start out with me gambling a meager $200 but winning $2000 on many occasions, my friends are my witnesses, but winning gave me a false sense of euphoria! I thought I could continue to win at the casinos of Atlantic City, and even considered investing in gambling school (learning to count cards) to increase my odds of winning, but as the saying goes "the house always wins"!

And, for several months, I attempted to prove that old adage wrong and win, but guess what? You guessed it, I lost more than I could afford! It got to the point where I was gambling $700 a week, and when I ran out of cash I tapped MAC, paying the extra finance charge for using the casino's machines, and I didn't stop there either! I became immune to the loss of dignity I felt the first time I used one of those Global Access counters that allow you to take a cash advance against a credit card, paying some exorbitant amount of money not hesitating using them even though I had to pay some hefty finance charge!

At first a few friends/family members and I would visit the casinos and just for fun, apply for the casino comp cards because they didn't cost us anything, but enabled us to get "free meals, show tickets, comps to Macy's, parking, and free hotel rooms," and we lapped it up like little puppies love milk, or should I say, I fell for it, hook, line and sinker.

The dinners, lunches and breakfasts were tasty, each casino offering its own delicacies, which I grew very fond of. The casinos could afford to hire the best chefs with all the money that is wasted there. I overheard someone use the analogy that gambling is like flushing your money down the toilet! Wow, for some unknown reason, this resonated with me, I wonder why?

Many times we would book hotel rooms with our comp dollars, but I would end up gambling all night long. I can remember a few times my friends slept, changed their clothing and came to escort me away from some black jack table. They were beginning to think that I had a gambling problem, along with my husband who was also becoming concerned with the new nasty bad habit I had developed.

This didn't deter me because I thought I would show them! Because I was retired and while everyone else was working, I started going to Atlantic City alone, during the day while my son was in school and my husband was working. I thought I'd run down there, strike it rich, or at least make a few thousand dollars, but no such luck! I seemed to lose every time now. What happened to winning? It was as if my sneaking down A.C. or lying about my whereabouts jinxed my winnings. I would come home broke, and thoroughly disgusted! I mean, I always knew God was in charge, and, in fact, would pray to win. But, then even when I did win, I would typically give it back to the casino hoping to win some obscene amount of money! Boy, was I greedy or what?

It wasn't until later that I learned that the casino's actually track their clientele by their comp card usage and total dollars gambled. In the beginning I did get some fun out of the casinos even though nothing I received was free at all.

I paid for every meal I ate and every hotel room I slept in. Every time I gambled I jeopardized my own integrity being a child of God.

PURSUING REAL ESTATE

REAL ESTATE LICENSE

Unfulfilled being retired on disability, I am currently embarking on a second career. In 2005 I returned to the classroom and attended the Temple University Real Estate Institute where I obtained my realtor's license through perseverance, and now am a practicing Real Estate Agent with Weichert Realtors First Realty Group in Philadelphia, Pennsylvania, where Darryl Miller is the Broker.

BRIDGET'S CLUES TO SOLVING HER PUZZLE OF LIFE

CHAPTER XXII

"I have come as a light to shine in this dark world, so that all who put their trust in me will no longer remain in the darkness."
John 12:46

FINDING THE CLUES

The theme of *Without a Clue* is that life for me was reminiscent of a jigsaw puzzle. "SYN - A puzzle as defined by Webster's New World College Dictionary, Fourth Edition implies such a baffling quality or such intricacy, as of a problem, situation, etc., that one has great difficulty in understanding or solving it."

My life was a conundrum, littered with trial and error and confusion because I am a student of life, and lacked a strong enough foundation to prevent me from many of the pitfalls I stumbled into. I unknowingly contributed to my very own misery and lack of joy because many of the emotions I chose to adapt were based on negative patterns I acquired along the way—secrecy, shame, low self-esteem, self hate, negativity and sadness which ultimately led me to be lost, isolated from others, afraid, in pain and very angry about my condition. . .

It wasn't until my diagnosis with Mixed Connective Tissue diseases that I decided to try to understand my life, dissecting the good from the bad, the known from the unknown, and assembling the pieces the best way I knew. My intention is to hopefully be a beacon of light to someone who may be as lost as I was, to serve God by sharing my truth, to reinforce what I believe to be, and to be an instrument believing that I was created to be my authentic self, as I leave my legacy for my children: Following are the clues which I have discovered:

- Spiritual Foundation,
- Confessing the Lord as Savior,
- Love God and Love Neighbor as Self—The Most important commandment
- Love One Another—Family and Friends
- Love Self—Developed better Self Image
- Hope and Faith—"As a Man Thinketh"—Attitude of Gratitude
- Truth-Sharing My Testimony-Increasing my Territory
- Better Steward of All that God has given Me
- God has a Plan—"My Steps are Ordered"
- My Heart's Desire.

CHAPTER XXIII

SPIRITUAL FOUNDATION—
LEAVING A LEGACY

In church when babies are christened at Enon, Pastor Waller customarily teaches that babies are born packed full of potential and that the role of his/her parents, godparents, and the village of believers that stand for him is to remind him who he is so that when he goes out into the world he will not forget the Lord. "Train up a child in the way he should go: and when he is old, he will not depart from it" (Proverbs 22:6).

Spiritually, I began my childhood journey at a major disadvantage, lacking the village of believers to set the spiritual foundation. There were no Bibles in our home, and the only praying we conducted was at bedtime reciting a memorized prayer: "Now thy lay me down to sleep, I pray the Lord my soul to keep, But, if I die before I wake, I pray the Lord my soul to take." And that was the extent of our religious preparation at home. My sister and I attended church with our maternal grandmother, we sang songs and recited Bible verses at Easter and Christmas time, yet our parents were void of knowledge pertaining to God, and in turn we all suffered from lack of knowledge!

My childhood recollection of God was a punishing God! I lived my entire life in fear of a loving God thinking He would strike me dead at any time for some infraction. I thought this simply because I didn't know any better. As we attended the church services, I hadn't yet grasped the meaning of prayer, and my mind would wonder "how much longer are we going to have to sit here and listen to mumble jumble or when are we going to eat" during the literal all day church service at the United Church of the First Born where you could count the attendees on both hands.

As I grew into my teenage years, I lived according to the ways of the world and participated in whatever seemed right at the time, sex outside of marriage, which led to fornication, which led to unwanted pregnancies, which led to terminations, keeping them a secret, and shame. All of which could have been prevented had I known who I was — "a child of God." Unfortunately, I felt alone in the world which made me an open target for the perilous pitfalls of Satan. I was blinded to my sinful nature and the world seemed to offer me instant gratification and happiness. Unbeknown to me, some of the things that I thought were good, were sinful, and kept me separated from Jesus Christ. I was in the mist of spiritual warfare and was clueless. "For we wrestle not against flesh and blood, but against principalities, against powers, against the rulers of the darkness of this world, against spiritual wickedness in high places" (Ephesians 6:12).

Fortunately, after my diagnosis, I inherited a village of

believers who have assisted me in beginning a new life in Jesus Christ, and have encouraged me to pray, give my burdens to the Lord and ask for God's protection and guidance. I made the choice to accept Jesus Christ as my Lord and Savior, and was baptized and received the right hand of fellowship. To God be the glory, I am still a work in progress, but I diligently try not to make my own choices for I have learned to lean on Him for all things.

DARKNESS

FEAR   PAIN

CONFUSION

SADNESS

LOST

SECRETS

QUIET

ANGER

HIDING

CHAPTER XXIV

CONFESSING LORD AS SAVIOR - BAPTISM

I was baptized for the second time in my life at Enon Tabernacle Baptist Church in Philadelphia, Pennsylvania, where I publicly confessed Jesus Christ as my Lord and personal Savior, and have been received into the full membership when I was baptized on February 27, 2007, in a momentous immersion along with my mother; accepted the call to worship with fellow believers at various church congregations and have benefited by attending several glorious retreats; opportunity to truly feel the love and support of family and friends, and opportunity to share the truth of my testimony.

The first time I accepted Christ I was just eleven years old, and I went along with Lisa, our cousin Marcy Newman, and other kids in our neighborhood because everyone else was getting baptized and it seemed like a fun thing to do because it was on Christmas Eve! Unfortunately, I didn't comprehend what it meant to be saved at that young age because had I known, I would have prayed for faith, strength, and courage for God to help guide me through the travails of life when our home was repossessed, and my parents lost their minds! The only way I know we survived was that God was in control and he carried us.

Before I was diagnosed with my dreaded illnesses, I was pretty wrapped up in unimportant trivial matters, and never imagined ever becoming sick! When I had my second son, David, I was extremely self-conscience about my appearance and wouldn't be caught without make-up! I remember a friend/sister-in-law, Jackie Houser, stopped by unannounced just to say "hello" and I "ran for cover" because I felt ashamed of the way I looked without my make-up. I had developed into a superficial monster. Jackie didn't care how I looked, she's my friend.

In retrospect, it seemed that I had to be at my lowest just to realize who I really am "a beloved child of God!"

Of course I would rather not have my condition, but if it means suffering a little now, but having my soul ascend to Heaven when I'm called home, I'll gladly accept my condition. In all actuality, my health issues have been a mixed blessing because I'm able to be a stay-at-home mom and see David III off to school in the morning and be home when he arrives home from school in the afternoon, spend quality time with my mother during the day driving her to doctor appointments, pharmacy visits, assist clients by helping them acquire the necessity of housing, as well as share my testimony in *Without A Clue*. I know the Lord has ordered my steps because I am able to do all of this as well as purchase my dream of a home.

The Lord is my shepherd; I have everything I need. He

lets me rest in green meadows; he leads me beside peaceful streams. He renews my strength. He guides me along right paths, bringing honor to his name. Even when I walk through the dark valley of death, I will not be afraid, for you are close beside me. Your rod and your staff protect and comfort me. You prepare a feast for me in the presence of my enemies. You welcome me as a guest, anointing my head with oil. My cup overflows with blessings. Surely your goodness and unfailing love will pursue me all the days of my life, and I will live in the house of the Lord forever.

Psalm 23:1–6

DARKNESS

FEAR   PAIN

CONFUSION

SADNESS

LOST

SECRETS

QUIET

ANGER

HIDING

CHAPTER XXV

LOVE GOD AND LOVE NEIGHBOR AS SELF—MOST IMPORTANT PIECES

Six years ago at age forty, during the most overwhelmingly painful era of my life, I received such a comforting message of security from three treasured friends, an inspirational card designed by Helen Steiner Rice, a lovely framed photo, and a table top ice memento all with the identical soothing passage of "Footprints." That last sentence enlightened me and gave me unimaginable joy "my precious child, I love you and would never leave you. During your times of trial and suffering, when you see only one set of footprints, it was then that I carried you."

Hallelujah! The enemy is defeated! Wow, "this was a light bulb moment for me," as Oprah would say and really caused me to think deeply. Immediately, as in the very first stanza of "Footprints", my mind rushed through the past, the skeletons (secrets) I kept buried, even from my closest friends, the emptiness I feel at times, the darkness that enveloped me day and night, the meaninglessness of it all, every single time I wrestle with overspending money, years of shame, the times I was afraid... am afraid... but, not anymore.

Suddenly, I see, no longer is my vision cloudy, I am clueless no more. The pieces of the puzzle begin to fall into place, and I am comforted because my spirit has been awakened and I realize I no longer walk alone.

FOOTPRINTS

One night a man had a dream. He dreamed he was walking along the beach with the Lord. Across the sky flashed scenes from his life. For each scene, he noticed two sets of footprints in the sand; one belonging to him, and the other to the Lord.

When the last scene of his life flashed before him, he looked back at the footprints in the sand. He noticed that at many times along the path of his life there was only one set of footprints. He also noticed that it happened at the very lowest and saddest times in his life.

This really bothered him and he questioned the Lord about it. "Lord, you said that once I decided to follow you, you'd walk with me all the way. But I have noticed that during the most troublesome times in my life, there is only one set of footprints. I don't understand why when I needed you most you would leave me."

The Lord replied, "My precious child, I love you and would never leave you. During your times of trial and suffering, when you see only one set of footprints, it was then that I carried you."

"Jesus replied, "The most important commandment is this: 'Hear, O Israel! The Lord our God is the one and only Lord. And you must love the Lord your God with all your heart, all your soul, all your mind, and all your strength. The second is equally important: 'Love your neighbor as yourself. No other commandment is greater than these." Mark 12:29–31 (NLT)

DARKNESS
FEAR   PAIN
CONFUSION
SADNESS
        LOST
SECRETS

            QUIET

ANGER

        HIDING

CHAPTER XXVI

LOVING ONE ANOTHER-FAMILY AND FRIENDS

I thank God for the gift of family and friends showing up daily, bestowing their love on me, and encouraging me to stay strong and not give up. Things were looking pretty bleak, but I was still alive, wasn't I, even after thinking I was going to die, and "God didn't bring me this far to leave me," my friend Mary would say! Mary was there with me now daily, washing my dirty laundry, supporting my immediate family, talking to the doctors, and reading me scripture. Why, I would question? Because she genuinely cared! She knew I was lost, scared, and extremely depressed. She was trying to bring light to a very dark place. During my sickness, we became extremely close, and I thank God for her. "All of you should be of one mind, full of sympathy toward each other, loving one another with tender hearts and humble minds" (1 Peter 3:8 NLT).

Mrs. Bosman would show up very early most mornings

now, like an angel without her wings, even before the slew of doctors made their a.m. visits, and I would light up because I was suffering from fear and shock all at once and felt so very alone and depressed about my situation. *How did she know they moved me to this isolated place and that I needed her so much*, I asked myself? I felt as though she empathized with me and was trying to keep me from sinking into that black hole that awaited me. She wiped every tear away as she comforted me, like she really was my true mother, and not only my ex-husband's mom. She truly loved me, and I felt it, and didn't dread going to sleep at night because I knew my angel would be there in the morning, whispering, "Good Morning little one." All these people are truly there for me! "We drive fear from our families and friends by loving one another so supportively that every one feels safe inside the group" (1 John 4:18).

But, thank God, it wasn't too late, because Jesus Christ changed the way I think from the inside out! "Instead, there must be a spiritual renewal of your thoughts and attitudes. You must display a new nature because you are a new person, created in God's likeness—righteous, holy, and true. But seek first his kingdom and his righteousness and all these things will be given to you as well" (Matthew 6:33).

My family and Christian friends (spiritual friends) were the catalyst to my recovery. At one of the scariest times in my life I was in the hospital, deeply depressed because either my fingertips had been amputated and I couldn't find my way or they were about to, and I could not imagine living without them, had lost faith, when all of a sudden my body tightened up and I was slumped over with my head bowed and literally couldn't raise my head. It felt like I was having an out-of-body experience! A few of my very close friends were visiting me, probably at the request of my husband, David, because he was baffled and didn't know what to do.

I vaguely remember Putt and Moriah (Putt had delivered her miracle baby, and my Godchild, Moriah, at age forty, and constantly had me in prayer and had prayer warriors make special visits to me in the hospital and at home. They came and talked with me as a group, and continued to pray for me. They put me on the sick and shut-in list at our church, West Oak Lane Church of God, so that everyone was able to pray for me) were there to try to braid my matted, very fragile hair into order, and to clean me up because it appeared that the nursing staff on duty were failing to ensure that I showered, not that I could blame them because I had regressed to believing that I couldn't walk again. Mary and Doris were there to pray, read scripture and sing me through this ordeal. Mary commanded, "Bridget, sit up, you don't sit that way!" But, my very weak response was "I can't." This scene honestly felt like something I had witnessed on television in the *Exorcist* with Linda Blair, but I was sitting in the chair playing the part of the very cursed Linda Blair with her eyes rolling around her head, and her head turning around her neck, throwing up green split pea soup! "What do you mean you can't," said Mary. She began to pray. Doris entered my very grieved hospital room smelling like she had just showered in her favorite Victoria Secret body wash awakening my senses and lighting up the room, and immediately began to join Mary in prayer, and began to read me scriptures. I distinctly remember she began by reading me the story of Job because of the similarity, and to give me hope because in the end God blessed Job with even more than he had lost. She also read Proverbs to me, while Mary began to clean me up.

"Bridget, do you have to go to the bathroom?"
"I can't walk!"
"You can walk, that was before!"
"Come on, I'll help you to use the restroom," she said as she gently nudged me up and guided me to the toilet. Once I finished in the bathroom, I remember both she and Doris helping me into bed, and turning on gospel music and praying me to sleep. This scene happened once in the hospital, and we could never quite label it. Mary thought it was an overdose of medication, but Doris thought it more like a deep depression, and I have to agree with her, and fortunately the darkness only lasted a few days, and not months, years or forever. I believe I lost faith temporarily, and my spirit was broken, but thank God my spiritual friends were there to pray me through.

Another very troubling event was a few Halloween's ago, I was, unfortunately, left at home alone after recently being discharged from the hospital. My husband took David to his family's house in Crestmont to go out for Halloween, and Mario was at work. I was okay while they were at home and it was light outside because if I wasn't okay they would have stayed at home to comfort me as they had always done. But, as soon as they left, a huge paranoia overtook me! I locked the door and turned off the lights, pretending as if no one was home, and attempted to sleep. But, as the children knocked on the door, I felt as though I were being attacked and tried to bury myself under the covers.

Once I went home from the hospital, I started attending church and retreats with my friends, including most of my hospital supporters, Doris, Patricia Burt, Putt, and the late Mrs. Bosman. They each worshipped at various churches, Mary at Enon Tabernacle, Doris at New Bethlehem,

Patricia at Bethel, Putt at West Oak Lane Church of God, and Mrs. Bosman worshipped at Mt. Airy Church of God. "So now I am giving you a new commandment; Love each other. Just as I have loved you, you should love each other. John 13:34.

DARKNESS

FEAR   PAIN

CONFUSION

SADNESS

LOST

SECRETS

QUIET

ANGER

HIDING

CHAPTER XXVII

LOVE SELF - DEVELOPED BETTER SELF IMAGE

"For as he thinketh in his heart, so is he" (Proverbs 23:7a New Scofield Bible). In order to develop my spiritual well being, I had to first pray and ask God to change my attitude from can't do to "can do." For Christ said in His word, "I can do all things through Christ which strengthens me" (Phil. 4:13). He broke the self-imposed barriers that I had placed in my mind.

Before I accepted Christ into my life I was my own worst enemy. I didn't feel good about myself in the least. I fought in my mind just to exist. I honestly loathed the girl in the mirror because I felt very inadequate. My hair was much too thin, my nose too wide, and I would literally pick myself apart with all the things that confirmed my negative viewpoint of myself. It took me hours to feel good enough to get out the door in the morning. I imagined that everyone felt good about themselves except me. The enemy was doing his job keeping me feeling discouraged and defeated. And, to put the icing on the cake, my dad often made derogatory remarks stereotyping all Black people, saying "we weren't capable of one thing or another." His comments often infuriated me because I was already having a tough time adjusting to who I was as an individual. I wasn't sure whether he thought himself unique from all other Black folk, whether he included my abilities in his generalizations, whether he hated himself and didn't think he was capable, or if he considered himself White and capable. I had a difficult time listening to his rhetoric and often challenged his opinion.

At some point, I had enough of my dad's putdowns, and whatever he thought about the entire race, because if what he said was true, I was doomed. I was determined to succeed in life, and hopefully, make my dad proud of me. I developed a thirst for knowledge, and adopted the attitude of becoming a life-long learner recognizing that in some areas where I am weak, there will be others who will offer support because they are stronger in that area. In addition, I became an avid reader and developed a strong interest in books pertaining to self-improvement. I learned to apply myself in my studies in high school, business school, and in college becoming the very first in my family to obtain a college degree. I didn't know then, but I do know now that it was the Grace of God that brought me from death to life. I had to discover my uniqueness and realize that God created me exactly the way he saw fit. As children we often recited, "God didn't make any junk." And, the scripture says, "And yet, Lord, you are our Father. We are the clay, and you are the potter; we are all formed by your hand." Isaiah 64:8

CHAPTER XXVIII

HOPE AND FAITH — "AS A MAN THINKETH" CRIPPLED PHYSICALLY (FAITH IN JESUS)

According to author James Allen, As a Man Thinketh, www.cornerstonebooks.net, "a man can only rise, conquer, and achieve by lifting up his thoughts. He can only remain weak, and abject, and miserable by refusing to lift up his thoughts." I decided to "see my glass as half-full rather than half-empty" and extrapolate the goodness and meaning in my diagnosis.

Physically, when faced with the condition of not being able to walk, I had to quit feeling sorry for myself long enough to take the focus off of Bridget, and to realize that my children needed me at home and that if I could help it, I would choose to walk again with God's help. I began believing and having faith that I would walk contrary to what it looked like. "What is faith? It is the confident assurance that what we hope for is going to happen. It is the evidence of things we cannot yet see" (Hebrews 11:1). I wouldn't accept being confined to a wheelchair for the rest of my life because I had too much work to do! Feeling hopeless and defeated was over. I simply had to reprogram my mind to believe I could walk again with God's help, a little hard work and determination, similar to the Serenity Prayer often recited in 12 step programs,

> "God grant me the Serenity to accept the things I cannot change... Courage to change the things I can and Wisdom to know the difference." "It is better to enter heaven with only one hand than to go into the unquenchable fires of hell with two." Mark 9:43–44

CHAPTER XXIX

TRUTH-SHARING MY TESTIMONY - INCREASING MY TERRITORY

On October 5, 2001, while still in the hospital adapting to my circumstances, a friend and former manager, who had her turn at mentoring me throughout my career, Bernadette Gant-Jones along with her husband Thurman presented my husband and me with a book, entitled *The Prayer of Jabez, Breaking Through to the Blessed LIFE*. It was definitely a thoughtful gift and because Bernadette had frequently encouraged me, suggesting I apply for positions, enroll in a particular course, or offered motherly wisdom, I felt there had to be something intrinsically special about the beautifully crafted book with the lovely illustrations. Instinctively, I sensed that this book had meaning and excitedly began to delve into its contents. The story is about a little-known Bible hero named Jabez, who prays "a four-part prayer that brings him extraordinary measure of divine favor, anointing, and protection. With great insight and practical application, the author helps readers discover how to release God's same miraculous power and experience the blessings God desires to give them."

Mary and I read and reread the book from cover to cover and began reciting the prayer that went like this:

> Now Jabez was more honorable than his brothers, and his mother called his name Jabez, saying, "Because I bore him in pain." And Jabez called on the God of Israel saying, "Oh, that You would bless me indeed, and enlarge my territory, that Your hand would be with me, and that You would keep me from evil, that I may not cause pain!" So God granted him what he requested.
>
> 1 Chronicles 4:9–10

I believe God has significantly impacted my life by increasing my territory, allowing me to be blessed and be a blessing to others because wherever I go I am able to tell of the mighty power of Jesus. Look at me, I exclaim, "Six years ago I was unable to walk, much less feed myself, but now I am a testament because Jesus is in the miracle business. I had chosen to give in to the enemy and give up." I recall a friend, Selma Cooper, presented me with a cracked souvenir cup with the inscription, "believe in miracles, they happen everyday." At that dismal time I thought, *I don't know what she means because it's over for me, I'm doomed. I encountered relatives and acquaintances who knew me when I felt cute, especially when I dolled myself up, but now I couldn't help but look awful and barely recognizable.*

But, as time progressed, I began getting the word of God into my spirit by reading my Bible and not just the many inspirational books I read on a monthly basis. David would say, "Bridget, I don't know why you're reading so many books, all you need to do is read the Bible. Would you just pick up the Bible?" As time progressed, I renewed my strength in the Lord. I prayed, asked God for forgiveness of any sins I may have done, read my Bible, praised the Lord, listened to spiritual songs, and had ministers and saints of God pray over me. I retell my testimony over and over again and prayerfully, impact lives. I have decided to join the Enon Helping Hand Ministry Family helping to feed and clothe the homeless. It's humbling knowing that "there but for the grace of God go I," in other words, I or any family member could be homeless. At one point in my mom's life, she was not in her right mind, and homeless, but that will never ever be again as long as I can help it.

DARKNESS

FEAR   PAIN
   CONFUSION
SADNESS
      LOST
SECRETS

            QUIET

ANGER

       HIDING

CHAPTER XXX

BETTER STEWARD OF WHAT GOD HAS GIVEN

Recently I registered for a ten week financial workshop conducted at ENON to begin the long process of reducing my credit card debt and out-of-control spending habits. I decided it was time, and that this workshop would be a great first effort for me! The forum was great because there were at least thirty other participants, each of whom had his/her own financial challenges, and our agreement was not to repeat anything that we shared personally during our meeting times. In addition, I was very inspired last season when Oprah unveiled her "Debt Diet, and especially felt inspired by the Bradley Family, Lisa and Steven, as they came out to their family/friends on national television in an effort to reduce their enormous $170,000 debt and start a savings account for their future." It is amazing how we all keep our challenges to ourselves for fear of "anyone finding out."

As hope for our current situations, the facilitators had at some point been sitting in the very seats we were sitting in and had volunteered to provide guidance, support, and to help guide us along the path to credit card freedom. Many of us had excessive amounts of credit card debt. However, the good news is that just as our facilitators recovered by developing strategies and techniques paying off their debt, changing their spending/habits, curtailing spending, keeping their hard earned money in their pockets, we had this same opportunity to turn our finances around.

As I stated previously in the book, I have a long history of being in financial bondage ever since I can remember, but what I came away from the seminar with was a tool, if I would learn to be more disciplined and accountable to God for how I spent money, I could recover from years of wasteful living, and in time I would recover from my frivolousness.

I discovered that I had been a poor steward of many of the resources God entrusted to me, including money, time and talent, and that it all belongs to God anyhow. Stewardship as defined by Webster's New World College Dictionary, Fourth Edition. "is a person morally responsible for careful use of money, time, talent or other resources, esp. with respect to the principles or needs of the community or group"

Finances—I never gave regularly in church, and tithing was out of the question. I was extremely wasteful and didn't believe in budgeting or living within my means. So, becoming a better steward has been a total adjustment for me because throughout my lifetime saving wasn't even a consideration, because I would have ended up spending my withdrawing the little I would have amassed. My style of living has been to purchase whatever saw fit to because I felt I never made enough to live the way I desired, therefore, my theory was to not deprive myself any further. However, this way of living definitely goes against biblical principles. Romans 13:8 says "pay all your debt, except the debt of love for others. You can never finish paying that! If you love your neighbor, you will fulfill all the requirements of God's law."

Time—Better Mother—The biggest misuse of my time has been not allocating ample quality time to my children. When Mario was younger, I was busy pursuing a college education in the evenings in hopes of creating a better life for us, and on the weekends, satisfying my desire for male companionship. Fortunately, Mario never lacked friends, especially since my brother Geneis resided with us. However, he did lack proper quality time with me, especially since I was a single-parent and considered myself "not-maternal." I have ample time to spend with David, and my goal is to carve out sufficient bonding time for our relationship to develop further. Hopefully, I will be effective in this endeavor. At times, I am inclined to relinquish my quality time with him to allow his dad to spend excessive time with him.

LUPUS SUPPORT GROUP AND FUNDRAISER

I joined a Lupus Support Group, sponsored by the Lupus Foundation of America, Inc. "Living Well with Lupus" is an annual symposium for people living with Lupus and other autoimmune diseases. Currently, they are in their fifth year of holding symposiums, where they bring together people living with Lupus, their families and a panel of experts to share the latest information to help individuals live well—or better—with Lupus. Current topics include: Advances in Research and Treatment, Lupus and the Brain, Let's

Think about it, Reproductive Health, How to Interpret Your Lab Results, Integrative Nutrition and Medicine, and Cardiovascular Disease in Lupus.

The first year I recruited my husband, stepmother, and Mary to accompany me, and we were surprised at the number of people with Lupus, and we learned a lot. Mary and her friend Lorraine were inspired to "Walk for the Cure," especially since I couldn't walk for myself.

SYSTEMIC LUPUS ERYTHEMATOSUS SELF-HELP (SLESH) COURSE

A new self-help course, a seven-week standardized program designed to teach people with Lupus how to take a more active part in their health care and live better with chronic disease, was sponsored by the Pennsylvania Department of Health.

Weekly sessions were facilitated by a team of trained volunteers and includes topics such as: basic medical information about Lupus, exercise, fatigue management, medication and treatments, doctor-patient communication and relaxation and stress management and more!

TALENT - LUPUS LOOP

In 2005 I organized a special team of family and friends (Team Bridget) to walk with me in my personal fight against Lupus in the Lupus Loop, sponsored by the Lupus Foundation of America. In our first year "Team Bridget" raised $1500 for Lupus research to help find the cure.

CHAPTER XXXI

"You didn't choose me. I chose you. I appointed you to go and produce fruit that will last, so that the Father will give you whatever you ask for, using my name."
John 15:16 (NLT)

GOD HAS A PLAN, "ORDERED MY STEPS"

Because of much adversity and the numerous afflictions I have encountered along my journey through life culminating with the past ten years of challenge and struggle, I am so much stronger, wiser, and full of hope because of every enduring experience. I have learned to place my faith in our Lord and Savior, Jesus Christ, "and we know that God causes everything to work together for the good of those who love God and are called according to his purpose for them" (Roman 8:28 NLT), as He has ordered our steps, orchestrating the time and season for what He desires to accomplish in our lives. I have discovered that it's impossible to have a new beginning without first going through an ending of sorts, no matter how bleak or jarring. In fact, I believe you gain more insight and growth when faced with the more challenging situations. Initially, I opposed changing situations that seemed to slight me. However, wisdom has taught me that "things are not always what they seem," and to expect more growth, embrace change, and prepare to be enlightened.

I realize I am blessed and have benefited from the Lord's protection and would have given up much too soon. At my lowest point, when there was no where else to turn, I have learned to depend on God. "For I know the thoughts and plans I have for you, says the Lord, thoughts and plans for welfare and peace and not for evil, to give you hope in your final outcome." Then you will call upon Me, and you will come and pray to Me, and I will hear and heed you. Then you will seek Me, inquire for, and require Me (as a vital necessity) and find me when you search for me with all your heart" Jeremiah 29:11–13 (AMPLIFIED BIBLE).

CHAPTER XXXII
―――――――――

MY HEART'S DESIRE

I feel blessed, similar to that of Job in the "second half of his life even more than in the beginning." Job 42:12. I have been able to achieve many of the goals I have set for myself and my family, including publishing my memoir, being sure to give God all the honor and glory for this major life accomplishment, which I've been contemplating since high school in 1975; developed a more intimate and loving relationship with David and my children, Mario and David III; sustained health by attempting to alter my nutrition and exercise wherever possible; developed a fuller spiritual life, with a deeper understanding of the Word of God, and have begun a relationship with Christ recognizing that as the songwriter sings, " He walks with me, and talks with me, along life's narrow way; He lives, He lives, Christ Jesus lives today, ask me how I know He lives, He lives within my heart;" and over a year ago August, the Lord has blessed us to be able to relocate in spite of my past credit challenges! I went to work in the real estate industry to as my husband, David, so eloquently stated "find myself a house" and that's precisely what has occurred.

Initially, I took courses at Temple University's Real Estate Institute to accompany Doris and to occupy my free time, obtained my license to practice real estate in Pennsylvania, and one thing led to another, I met a client, Harry Johnson, who inspired me to invest. Harry said, "Bridget, instead of getting a home equity loan to pay off credit card debt that you end up charging up again or spending, invest in a house." Well, he didn't have to tell me twice! I shared my insight with my husband, David, who it seemed had been sitting on the fence to homeownership for the eight years we had been married, and we began searching for a house, and fortunately, and with God's help we found the perfect home for our family, and a bonus is that it's located in an exceptional school district for David III, Abington, which happens to be the same school district my husband, David, attended throughout his lifetime and graduated from twenty-eight years ago. In addition, we were even able to keep Limekiln Pike, which Mario, who is now twenty-two years old, resides in. What a mighty powerful plan God had! For years I couldn't see it. Reflecting back, my husband wanted me to sell it, I bought him out and lived in it all my adult life, but didn't enjoy living in it, I changed my attitude about living in it, invested in it by refurbishing the entire house, inside and out, and finally, the Lord said, "Well done, my good and faithful servant."

Without a Clue is my testimony of my journey to God. Unfortunately, it took a health crisis, an inability for me to walk for a period of well over a year and my developing chronic health conditions in order for me to get in touch with the truth and develop an understanding of life and be transformed mentally, physically, financially and spiritually. Throughout my lifetime, I, like many of you, have had to overcome many challenging situations which initially left me wounded, confused and joyless because I was young and inexperienced. I felt defeated as I lived in utter darkness, fear, shame, aloneness and financial bondage for well over forty years simply because I had no idea Jesus Christ resided within me! I have discovered life to be a complex puzzle, a process (a continuing development involving many changes), totally unsolvable without the clues of faith, hope, and love, which take us through doom to enlightenment woven together to intertwine all the pieces of the puzzle together, and be illuminated by the truth, way and love of Jesus Christ. *There are three things that will endure-faith, hope and love-and the greatest of these is love (*1 *Corinthians* 13:11–13, NLT*).*

DARKNESS

FEAR   PAIN

   CONFUSION
SADNESS
            LOST

SECRETS

                QUIET

ANGER

         HIDING

CHAPTER XXXIII

EPILOGUE

When I retired on disability in 2001 I was in a sad state, because I didn't want to retire, I had no choice, my health was on the decline and it was the only option I had. However, my co-workers got together and sent me a lovely inspirational plaque to encourage me to not give up hope, but to get up and live! It reads,

"The Power of Attitude"
"Our lives are not determined by what happens to us, but by how we react to what happens; not by what life brings to us, but by our attitude we bring to life. A positive attitude causes a chain reaction of positive thoughts, events, and outcomes. It is a catalyst ... a spark that creates extraordinary results."

I have gleaned so much wisdom from my life experiences, both good and bad. However, my failures and seeming catastrophes have been the truest teachers of them all.

I have written my life story in an attempt to gain added

clarity, to purge some of my own pent-up baggage which I have transported around for far too many years. My goal was to rid myself of the waste so that I would have space for the hope, joy, love and peace that's available to us when we desire it! "I have learned that when I open up to others, others open up to meet me, and then the journey isn't that bad."

"Without a Clue" by no means contains all of the answers, however, I have given just a snapshot of my life, going against the grain of a few individuals who may have felt "some things were best left unsaid." However, authentically I feel compelled to share from the core of my soul, and more importantly, connect with others who may be struggling with some of the very same issues I've encountered along the way.

I hope that you have seen glimpses of your own life story, propelling you to write. May God continue to bless you as you "let your light shine" and expect nothing less than hope, pure joy, peace, love and blessings!

"Weeping may go on all night, but joy comes with the morning" (Psalms 30:5).

SELECTED BIBLIOGRAPHY

Ban Breathnach, Sarah. *Excavating Your Authentic Self.* New York: Warner Brothers, 1998.

Cheek, Jonathan. *Conquering Shyness, The Battle Anyone Can Win.* Reed Business Information, 1989.

Frazier, George. *Success Runs in our Race: The Complete Guide to Effective Networking in the Black Community.* William Morrow and Company, Inc., 2004.

Warren, Richard. *The Purpose Driven Life: What On Earth Am I Here For?* Grand Rapids, Michigan: Zondervan, 2002.

Peck, M. Scott, MD. *The Road Less Traveled.* New York: Touchstone, 1978.

Tracy, Brian. *Create Your Own Future: How to Master the 12 Critical Factors of Unlimited Success.* Hoboken, NJ: John Wiley & Sons, Inc., 2002.

Vanzant, Iyanla. *Until Today: Daily Devotions for Spiritual Growth and Peace of Mind.* New York: Fireside, 2000.

Gills, James P. M.D. *Imaginations: More than you Think.* Lake Mary, Florida: Creation House Press, 2004.

Gray, John, PhD. *How to Get What You Want and Want What You Have: A Practical and Spiritual Guide to Personal Success.* New York: Harper Collins Publishers, 1999.

Bruch, Hilde, M.D. *Learning Psychotherapy: Rationale and Ground Rules.* Cambridge, Massachusetts: Harvard University Press, 1974.

Hill, Napoleon. *Think and Grow Rich.* Fawcett Columbine, 1986.

Miedaner, Talane, *Coach Yourself to Success:* 101 *Tips from a Personal Coach for Reaching Your Goals at Work and in Life.* Lincolnwood (Chicago), Illinois: Contemporary Books, 2000.

Kent, Margaret. *How to Marry the Man of Your Choice.* Warner Press, 1988.

McGraw, Philip C. *Life Strategies: Doing What Works, Doing What Matters.* Mass Market Paperback, 2000.

Wilkinson, Bruce. *The Prayer of Jabez, Breaking Through to the Blessed Life.* Colorado Springs: Multnomah Publishers, Inc., 2000.

Web MD Medical Reference from Healthwise @ 1995–2007, Healthwise, Inc.